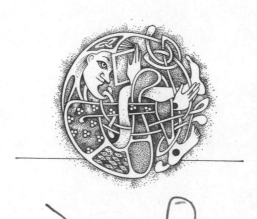

Donald F Power

Labor Agreement in Negotiation and Arbitration

Labor Agreement
IN Negotiation
AND Arbitration

Arnold M. Zack
Richard I. Bloch

The Bureau of National Affairs, Inc., Washington, D.C.

Second Printing March 1984

Library of Congress Cataloging in Publication Data

Zack, Arnold.
  The labor agreement in negotiation and arbitration.

  Includes bibliographies and index.
    1. Collective labor agreements—United States.
I. Bloch, Richard I.   II. Title.
KF3408.Z3   1983   344.73′0189   83-2552
                      347.304189

International Standard Book Number: 0-87179-398-9
Printed in the United States of America

Preface

A collective bargaining agreement is a unique document. It is a contract that, in the traditional sense of the term, attempts to reduce to writing the mutually intended goals of the parties. But there are numerous distinctions applicable to this labor-management document. Unlike other contracts, for example, it is intended not as a codification of a one-time allegiance but rather as a broad set of mutually agreed upon provisions applicable to a continuing relationship. Unlike other contracts, it is far reaching in its attempt to regulate the conduct of a number of individuals, perhaps even hundreds or thousands, on one hand, and a corporate entity, on the other. And the breach of this agreement leads, in the usual case, not to a severance of the relationship but to a remedy that seeks to assure its continuation.

It is an accepted truism that no two parties can hope to regulate every aspect of their relationship in any written document; in the final analysis, the good faith of the contracting parties, and their respective willingness to establish a workable relationship, is the controlling factor. But disputes will inevitably occur. The ability to resolve them effectively and economically depends on the parties' sophistication in drafting the agreement and in implementing it.

This book is intended as a guide to understanding the labor agreement so as to assist parties in its formulation and administration. The materials that follow scrutinize the innards of the labor agreement. While the initial chapter briefly examines the theoretical nature of the labor agreement, the greater part of the text is more pragmatic in nature. The attempt herein is to provide the labor relations student and practitioner with an overview as to the impact and intent of various aspects of the labor agreement.

In order to highlight the various questions that may arise, we have chosen to examine the agreement on a section-by-section basis. Each chapter includes a general overview intended to set forth the purposes and problems of a given provision. We have also included a series of discussion cases and comments throughout the text and a list of suggested readings at the end of the book designed to provoke thinking and/or discussion on some of the more troublesome aspects of the particular subject.

The cases are, for the most part, real. They have been "sanitized" at times to account for privacy and confidentiality considerations, but they nevertheless raise issues that must be, and have been, taken seriously by practitioners.

After an initial view of what a labor contract is, we turn to discussions of generally accepted principles, or rules, of contract interpretation, including a brief statement on questions of evidence in the context of labor arbitration. Chapter 3 then turns to a discussion of an increasingly important consideration for both those who draft and those who interpret contracts—the impact of external law. Here we review the long, and at times fervent, debate on whether and to what extent arbitrators should be bound by public laws in a private tribunal; whether and to what extent the arbitral process should be modified to accommodate the realities of outside law and the relationship between the arbitration forum and external agencies in terms of deferral to the respective opinions. This section closes with a review of public sector labor relations where, more than anywhere else, external law becomes an everyday consideration.

We then turn to a review of the contract provisions themselves. Labor agreements are custom tailored documents. They differ greatly according to parties' individual needs. We have concentrated on the most significant and pervasive sections. Implementation of a grievance procedure and seniority rights are generally regarded as organized labor's most important contributions, from a contractual standpoint, and we have devoted considerable space to those provisions. Similarly, while disciplinary matters are often seen merely as fact questions or the proper application of "just cause," the contractual basis of discipline in the labor relations context may hardly be overlooked. Accordingly, we devote a chapter to that subject.

The overwhelming influence of the authors' mentors and arbitrator friends must not be ignored. While they may have had no direct input into the pages of this volume, the authors' thoughts, responses, and their overall view of arbitration have been meaningfully molded and refined by these people. David P. Miller and Saul Wallen were the long-time mentors to Bloch and Zack. Each man was directly responsible as a teacher and guide and promoter in our respective careers. Their generosity, tough-mindedness, and passionate love for the institution of arbitration left to us and to the profession a valued legacy.

The authors also wish to express their gratitude to the several people who assisted meaningfully in this project. Margaret Clark and Robert Jones provided research and critical insight. Eileen Brookshire, Laurie Thompson, and Sharon Willier worked long hours typing the numerous drafts. Finally, our families have borne with grace and humor the many late-night phone calls, harried meetings, early-morning think sessions, and other unconscionable demands on what are otherwise highly rewarding family lives.

Arnold Zack
Boston, Massachusetts

Richard Bloch
Washington, D.C.

January 1983

Contents

The Contract Provisions

The "Rules" of Contract Interpretation

1

Theory of the Labor Agreement

As noted by numerous articles, treatises, and treatments on the subject, the concept of a collective bargaining agreement has been thoroughly reviewed in exhaustive detail. There is no ready consensus as to the theoretical foundation or precise legal status of the document. But it is clear beyond question that it is a powerful and significant agreement, both within the industrial forum and, when necessary, in the courts. In practice, the theories of its origin are less important than the scope and purpose of the individual contract and, within that document, the particular sections and phrases. But for a moment, it is appropriate to review some general theories on the legal status of the labor contract.

Professor Theodore St. Antoine has identified at least three themes and variations that have been employed over the years to explain the legal status of the labor contract.[1] First, the labor agreement may be seen as establishing local customs which are then incorporated into individual employees' contracts. Some view this as constituting two bilateral contracts —one for the union, which it may enforce on its behalf, and another for the benefit of the individual employees. The second theory is that the collective agreement is a bargain negotiated by the union as the employees' agent. And third, the labor agreement is defined by some courts as a third-party benefici-

---

[1] Smith, Merrifield, and St. Antoine, *Labor Relations Law: Cases and Materials* (Indianapolis: Bobbs-Merrill, 5th ed. 1974), at 758.

ary contract. The basic agreement is between the employer and the union for the benefit of the employee-beneficiary.

This smorgasbord of approaches was of primary importance in times when courts were struggling to determine theories upon which enforcement actions would be based. Today, labor agreements in industries affecting commerce are enforced under Section 301 of the Labor Management Relations Act. The Supreme Court has recognized that collective agreements are not "ordinary contracts" in the commercial sense, but are more properly regarded as generalized codes that serve as an overall constitution in a system of industrial self-government.

Archibald Cox has rejected any attempt to construct parallels between the collective bargaining agreement and contracts employed in the legal or commercial worlds.[2] Cox noted that general principles in this area should "not be imposed from above; they should be drawn out of the institutions of labor relations and shaped to their needs."[3]

As Professor David Feller has observed,[4] a true understanding of the nature of the collective bargaining agreement may be gained not by undue concern over its form but rather by careful attention to the function it was intended to perform. He stated:

> "If any generalization about collective bargaining agreements can safely be made, it is that until 1947, when Congress enacted Section 301 [of the Labor Management Relations Act] to give 'statutory recognition [to] the collective agreement as a valid, binding and enforceable contract,' . . . and indeed in most respects even after that, collective agreements were not negotiated with an eye to judicial remedies. The terms and the forms of such agreements represented a functional answer to the needs of the parties, formulated without any consideration of potential judicial intervention. The parties did not regard themselves as drafting agreements to be sued on by third party beneficiaries, or specifications like those in a tariff to be inserted into contracts of employment of individual employees, or any of the other contractual analogies which have, from time to time, been suggested.[5]

---

[2]Cox's two articles, "Rights Under a Labor Agreement," 69 *Harv. L. Rev.* 601 [1956], and "The Legal Nature of Collective Bargaining Agreements," 57 *Mich. L. Rev.* 1 [1958], are essential reading for any serious student of the subject.
[3]69 *Harv. L. Rev.* at 605.
[4]Feller's "A General Theory of the Collective Bargaining Agreement," 61 *Cal. L. Rev.* 663 (1973), is another important addition to the literature on the subject.
[5]*Id.* at 720. Citations omitted.

Feller identified three needs within an industrial system. First, there must be rules to guide the conduct of employees. Second, because workers must be relied upon to act in predictable ways, without minute and continuing direction, they must be willing to cooperate. Essential to cooperation is consistency in management, and the rules help to promote this as well. Finally, modern industrial organization demands bureaucratic organization and the labor agreement helps to establish the rules and limitations that must, of necessity, exist at varying levels of the management hierarchy. Thus, the final industrial collective bargaining agreement is not simply an agreement on the terms by which employees will work but rather a document covering rules to be observed in the management of all employees.

Clearly, the collective bargaining agreement is a remarkable document. It incorporates the party's own rules of conduct and operation, establishes a system of internal self-government, gives life to seniority, and even establishes certain rights that may endure beyond the termination of the document itself.

Critical to the purpose of this text is the recognition that contract formation is a process of "custom tailoring." Parties formulate collective agreements in response to particular needs—a fact that dare not be ignored by neutrals who become involved in the process for relatively brief periods.

In one significant respect, commercial and labor contracts are indistinguishable. They both seek to record parties' mutual agreements on various subject matters. The remainder of the first portion of this book is directed to general considerations in ascertaining that intent. Part II is devoted to the various forms the parties employ to express their intent, as well as potential problems and questions that may arise in the context of these endeavors.

2

General Principles of Contract Interpretation

The overall purpose of a labor agreement, like any other written agreement, is to establish the mutual intent of the contracting parties. Ideally, parties express themselves with such clarity and precision that the resulting document leaves nothing to the imagination. It is safe to say, however, that such an ideal is rarely met. Labor agreements are, after all, the product of bargaining. Language may well be the result of compromise as well as unskilled or careless drafting. Provisions may have been inserted quickly, in response to a strike situation or contract deadline. At times, clauses will have been intentionally drafted in a vague manner, either in the hope that a dispute will never arise in that area or with the knowledge that it will. In the latter case political necessities may well have led both parties to "leave it to the arbitrators."

The proper role of the arbitrator is to interpret and apply the labor agreement. If the language is clear, the arbitrator must tell the parties what it means, not what it should mean. As Dean Harry Shulman noted, the arbitrator does not exist to dispense his or her own brand of industrial justice. But disputes arise because language is not clear or because, while clear, the provision must be applied to an unanticipated set of circumstances. In cases where the labor agreement fails to provide the necessary guidance, there must be a set of rules for the contract reader to apply in attempting to interpret the document. Often, but not always, these rules parallel those es-

6

tablished in the context of nonlabor agreements, taken together with some practical realities relevant to the labor relations arena.

Plain Meaning

Parties are presumed to have meant what they said. Unless agreed otherwise, an arbitrator will enforce the terms as written. One party's contention that certain language was not intended to say what it says will be unpersuasive, particularly where the other side is content to refer the arbitrator to the "clear language of the agreement." It should be remembered, however, that, while clear, given language may not necessarily be applicable to the situation at issue.

Plain meaning has further significance. The so-called "plain meaning rule" holds that evidence beyond the four corners of the agreement should not be considered absent a finding that the language itself is somehow ambiguous. Arbitrators may not refashion the parties' agreement. Unfortunately, this overlooks the possibility that, in fact, the parties might have intended another meaning to the clause, despite inartful drafting. Should persuasive, albeit extrinsic, evidence be ignored in such circumstances? Judge Roger Traynor has stated:

> "The test of admissibility of extrinsic evidence to explain the meaning of a written instrument is not whether it appears to the court to be plain and unambiguous on its face, but whether the offered evidence is relevant to prove a meaning to which the language of the instrument is reasonably susceptible."[1]

There are numerous rules applied by the reader of a contract in order to resolve disputes over its meaning. Rules guide the contract reader to avoid nonsensical results and, in general, are modeled after what one would intuitively expect parties to be contemplating as they write the agreement. The adage "expressio unius est exclusio alterius"—for example, to express one thing is to exclude another—proceeds on the premise that if parties have listed certain elements, they have

---

[1]*Pacific Gas & Electric Co. v. G. W. Thomas Drayage Co.,* 69 Cal. 551, 442 P.2d 641 (1968), cited in Arbitrator Raymond Goetz's "Comment," in *Truth, Lie Detectors, and Other Problems in Labor Arbitration,* Proceedings of the 31st Annual Meeting, National Academy of Arbitrators (Washington, D.C.: BNA Books, 1979), at 221. See also the Uniform Commercial Code, Section 2–203, Comment 1(b).

included all elements they intended to consider. If something does not appear in the list, the assumption is the parties did not intend it to be there. This is entirely reasonable.

Another rule of interpretation seeks to resolve issues of ambiguous language. Where the question is whose side the language will favor, if there is no other guidance, the language will be interpreted against the party who drafted it. In essence, this serves to penalize that party for having written the language poorly. The assumption here is that, as between the two parties, the least innocent in this situation must assume the burden.

There are a number of other practical rules which deserve some further scrutiny.

Consistent versus Inconsistent

An arbitrator will proceed on the assumption that contracting parties intended a document to be consistent throughout. One assumes, therefore, that they did not intend to contradict what was established in one paragraph by means of a later provision.

A disputed contract provision may be clearly at odds with a provision elsewhere in the agreement. Nevertheless, the arbitrator's job is to apply that provision. It is for the parties to clean up, through negotiation, the obvious mess that may ensue. But if the provision may be interpreted in several ways, one of which is consistent with the rest of the agreement, arbitrators will accept that option. The consistency factor helps to explain further the intent of the contracting parties.

Standard versus Technical

In many industries, terms of art find their way into the labor agreement. The reason these words are important is that they have special meaning to the parties. But it is at times difficult to tell whether a particular term is being used in the "standard" sense or whether, instead, a "technical" or "artful" sense is intended. Parties are well advised to recognize that, unless otherwise specified, arbitrators will employ the standard or common sense meaning. Accordingly, if parties wish to rely on any other meaning, it is incumbent upon them to specifically so state.

Parol Evidence

The parol evidence rule, as applied to the labor agreement, means that the contract made by the parties is the final and binding document; it supersedes any tentative terms derived from earlier negotiations. This means that the labor agreement itself is the controlling document and the best evidence of the parties' intent. Evidence of contrary intentions expressed prior to, or contemporaneous with, the formation of the agreement, or of other agreements, will not be admissible. Note that the parol evidence rules applies to prior expressions of intent and does not prevent the parties from modifying the agreement subsequent to its formation. Thus, evidence as to the parties' subsequent actions or writings will be relevant and potentially significant.

Note, however, that the entire parol evidence rule hangs, in one sense, on a weak hook. As noted earlier, the "plain meaning rule," itself a form of the parol evidence rule, has been all but repudiated. One may understand what is required in terms of staying within the four corners of the agreement, yet, if the words are clearly ambiguous, the arbitrator may stray outside. And, as observed earlier, one party may generally present evidence to show that otherwise "plain meanings" are not so plain. Considering this, as well as the less rigid approach to rules of evidence in arbitration, one should scarcely place great weight on the parol evidence rule.

Past Practice

Arguments over past practice pervade the area of contract interpretation. This is because actual practice under an agreement may be considered as yielding reliable evidence as to what was meant by a particular provision.

The difficult situations arise in cases where practice is relied upon to contradict otherwise "clear" contract language or where there is no provision in question and the practice is suggested as supplementing the written contract so as to be binding on the parties. It is important to recognize that in cases where a party wishes to clothe past practice with contractual status, that practice must reflect as many of the elements of a contract as possible. In essence, the practice must be "the understood and accepted way of doing things over an extended period of time."[2] Moreover, it must be understood by the parties that there is an obligation to continue doing things this way in the future. This being the case, a "practice" known to just one side and not the other will not normally be considered as the type of mutually agreeable item that is entitled to arbitral enforcement. Arbitrator Sylvester Garrett has defined a practice in these words:

> "A custom or practice is not something which arises simply because a given course of conduct has been pursued by management or the employees on one or more occasions. A custom or a practice is a usage evolved by men as a normal reaction to a recurring type situation. It must be shown to be the *accepted* course of conduct characteristically repeated in response to the given set of underlying circumstances. This is not to say that the course of conduct must be *accepted* in the sense of both parties having agreed to it, but rather that it must be *accepted* in the sense of being regarded by the men involved as the *normal* and *proper* response to the underlying circumstances presented."[3]

Moreover, practice is the product of a particular set of circumstances. Arbitrators have uniformly held that when those circumstances change, the practices surrounding them may also change. That is a critical (and logical) distinction between practice and the labor agreement.

—— Case ——

Jaye Morgan worked as a Grade 6 assembler in an aircraft parts plant. However, her skills were less

---

[2] These are the words of Richard Mittenthal, whose article "Past Practice and the Administration of Collective Bargaining Agreements," in *Arbitration and Public Policy*, Proceedings of the 14th Annual Meeting, National Academy of Arbitrators (Washington, D.C.: BNA Books, 1961), at 30, is the most thoughtful and comprehensive discussion of the subject.
[3] 2 *Steelworkers Arb. Bull.* 1187 (1953), as quoted in Mittenthal, *supra* note 2, at 31.

than satisfactory and she consistently failed to meet the standard level of output. Accordingly, management disqualified her from that position and downgraded her to a Grade 5 bench hand job.

The union grieved, contending that in every instance wherein employees had been disqualified, they were allowed to transfer laterally into other Grade 6 jobs. There were no exceptions. Management responds that, while a practice had, indeed, developed, all instances occurred after Morgan's case. Thus, at the time she was disqualified, there was no such practice.

Question and Comment

(1) *How should the arbitrator decide?*

The answer here depends on the arbitrator's view of the practice. If, in fact, it may be seen as an accurate reflection of the contracting parties' intent, then the grievant should prevail, even though the cited practice had not surfaced earlier. But if lateral transfers were first implemented as a "way of doing things" after Morgan's case, the situation would be different. Even if, at some later date, one might claim the practice binding, such impact had not been felt at the time of the Morgan case.

—— Case ——

From 1940 to 1968, U.S. Timber Products was located in the midst of a large city. It maintained a parking lot below its building, and employees could park free of charge. In 1968, however, the employer moved to another location that did not include parking. It was necessary for employees to park in a commercial lot and thereby incur parking charges of $6 per day. They grieved, contending that, as a matter of past practice, the employer had always provided cost-free parking.

Questions and Comments

(1) *What resolution?*

This case well reflects a situation where practice is tied to circumstances. When the employer had a parking facility available, employees could utilize it. This, however, did not amount to an obligation to pay parking expenses as an element of compensation, unless such was negotiated. When the circumstances changed—parking space was no longer available—so did the practice surrounding them.

(2) *Would the answer be different if the employer had previously reimbursed employees for parking charges?*

On the one hand, an arbitrator may conclude that this practice had been mutually approved and consistently implemented. It was therefore the type of unwritten promise that was to be considered as the effective equivalent of contract language. It thereby became enforceable by the arbitrator. But what if the labor agreement contained the contractual restriction on arbitrator's authorities to the extent that "the arbitrator shall not alter, amend, or add to the terms of the labor agreement"? In finding that the past practice had satisfied the various requirements (mutually agreed upon, clearly known to both parties, etc.), the arbitrator would be concluding that such practice had become part of the contract. This is, of course, a type of legal fiction but will nevertheless be relied upon by some neutrals in order to enforce what has been found to be a clear element of the parties' labor relationship.

Past practice also arises in a somewhat different form in the disciplinary context. Assume, for example, that the employer routinely allows individuals to report for work up to five minutes late without being docked. Then, one person is disciplined in some form or other for a late check-in of five minutes. The union grieves, contending that, as a matter of past practice, this had not been considered misconduct. This is a variation of the past practice argument. In a less direct but no less compelling manner, this custom and practice has become a part of the labor agreement under the "just cause" requirement. If it had, indeed, been the agreed-upon way of doing things, albeit tacitly, then the employer may not change the rules of the game in this manner. Note, however, that this "practice" is more in the nature of condonation than a direct employment benefit. While just cause may not be present in the particular case cited above, arbitrators have long sustained the employer's right to reverse the condonation process by serving notice that, henceforth, existing rules will be enforced. This, then, is to be distinguished from situations such as the parking lot case, where practices in the nature of clear contractual benefits may, in the appropriate circumstances, be required to be maintained.

A final caveat is in order. Proving a practice can be difficult in the extreme. This is understandable; these are the problems of proving any unwritten agreement.

Problems of Proof—Evidence in Arbitration

Perhaps the only predictable element in an arbitration hearing is that there will be an argument over evidence. It is not clear whether this is due to too many lawyers or too few, whether, instead, it arises from the occasional mix of lawyers and nonlawyers. Some say the half-formal, half-informal nature of the proceedings is at the heart of the problem. Were it clearly a legal proceeding or clearly not, all would know the rules, it is argued. Perhaps, on the other hand, arguments exist simply because the process is adversarial.

For whatever reason, substantial blocks of valuable hearing time are spent arguing admissibility and weight of various pieces of evidence. The intent here is to provide some views and overviews with respect to evidence in arbitration. One would be naive to believe that ironclad answers will result from this discussion. However, to the extent these principles are seen as guidelines, they may well assist parties in utilizing the hearing process to resolve problems instead of creating them.

One must immediately confess to a bias that may be self-evident. The very act of discussing rules of evidence suggests they have a place in an arbitration hearing. This means the arbitrator will be serving to filter, to a certain extent, materials proffered by the parties in support of their respective cases. It is here that one must part company with those who simply refuse to make evidentiary rulings—who routinely prefer, instead, to "let it in for what it's worth." One proceeds with recognition of Clare McDermott's Presidential Address to the National Academy of Arbitrators in 1980, where he warned that "litigation and its formalistic trappings are for dead and dying relationships, whereas arbitration is for living ones." He noted:

> "It could be dangerous to arbitration's health if some practitioners were to succeed in transplanting techniques suitable to the law into arbitration, without very careful and critical analysis."[4]

There is no reason to quarrel with the notion that arbitration dare not elevate the form of the presentation over its substance. To do so would, as McDermott observes, challenge its vitality. Nevertheless, no matter how informal the hearing process, there comes a time when it is unsatisfactory and potentially unfair to deny the parties guidance on the use to which the arbitrator intends to put certain proffered materials. To be sure, many disputed points may reasonably be glossed over by the neutral with the wholly defensible intent of progressing to hear the essence of the case. Many points will have no impact on the case; time spent in wrestling with niceties of admissibility is better spent moving on with the case. But there are also times when a particular piece of evidence becomes undeniably critical, when "letting it in for what it's worth" is unfair because the parties must reasonably be told, then and there, what indeed that evidence is worth. This is not to say that the arbitrator must disclose the weight a given portion of the evidence may have. Yet, the parties should not be surprised by learning, for the first time, in the opinion that evidence has or has not been admitted. A key document submitted in lieu of an absent witness may well require a definitive ruling. If the

---

[4]In *Decisional Thinking of Arbitrators and Judges*, Proceedings of the 33rd Annual Meeting, National Academy of Arbitrators (Washington, D.C.: BNA Books, 1981), at 18.

holding is that the contents would be accepted as the functional equivalent of testimony, then the offering party may forego the time and expense of securing the individual witness. At the same time, the other party should be well advised not to rely on the arbitrator's later discounting that material as, for example, hearsay; the immediate search for rebuttal materials may be essential.

What follows here is a review of some of the most common evidentiary questions that arise in arbitration. In no sense should one infer that the goal of this examination is to endorse more formal or legalistic hearings. To the contrary, arbitration continues to function as an important internal dispute settlement procedure precisely because of its ability to provide an informal and flexible forum for the airing of disputes. The point to be made, instead, is that arbitrators and the parties must not sacrifice basic fairness in the name of informality. When a question arises concerning evidence, it should be answered. Hopefully, a general understanding of the reasons behind the rules will enable parties to proceed with a clearer view of the fact-finding process.

The underlying reason for rules of evidence is to attempt to construct machinery by which the reliability of evidence may be tested. Firsthand, direct evidence is better than secondhand, originals are better than carbons, recollections recorded at the time of the event are presumed to be better than those revisited at a later time.

Most arbitration hearings involve one or more of the following types of evidence:

- Live testimony
- Affidavits
- Depositions
- Personnel records
- Pictures and tapes
- Doctor's slips
- Transcripts
- Rulings of outside agencies (courts, unemployment compensation boards, etc.)

In this chapter, each of these will be examined with an eye toward the potential and practical problems at arbitration. Then we turn to a related question involving the nature and extent of the discovery process in arbitration. However, before reviewing the individual elements of evidence, it is appropriate that we discuss the rule that cuts across numerous evidentiary questions and which, indeed, engenders more disputes than any other.

Hearsay

One standard definition of hearsay is as follows:

"Hearsay evidence is live testimony, or written evidence, of a statement made 'out of court,' the statement being offered as an assertion to show the truth of the matters asserted therein, and thus resting for its value upon the credibility of the 'out-of-court' asserter. Stated otherwise, hearsay is second-hand evidence submitted for the same purpose as if it were first-hand. (Did you see Joe hit Sam? Answer: No, I *heard* someone *say* that Joe hit Sam.)"[5]

One may well believe that the witness heard someone report the fight. But beyond this, we do not know, even assuming he actually heard the report, whether the fight occurred. Thus, for proving the truth of the matter—whether there was a fight—the testimony is of limited value.

Does this mean it is inadmissible? Not necessarily. Again, it depends whether the evidence is being submitted "for proving the truth of the matter asserted." If the testimony is submitted to prove there was a fight, then an objection should be sustained. The parties sponsoring the witness in this case should know, then and there, that the arbitrator will not base his or her decision as to the existence of a fight on such testimony. The opposing side should know that it need not defend that claim, at least at this point, since the arbitrator is ruling that this does not constitute proper evidence of the alleged offense.

However, as suggested above, there are purposes for which such testimony may be admitted. If the question is: "Why did the supervisor begin an investigation," it is perfectly

---

[5] *McCormick on Evidence* (St. Paul, Minn.: West, 1972), Sec. 246, at 584. See also *Wigmore on Evidence* (Boston: Little, Brown, 1974), Vol. 5, at ¶1361, 6 *id.* at 1766. Scholars often debate the distinction between a statement that is admissible because it is not hearsay and one that, while hearsay, is admissible because it is an exception to the hearsay rule. For present purposes, however, we classify all "out-of-court" statements as "hearsay," inquiring only as to whether they should be admitted as an exception.

proper for the supervisor to respond that a report of a fight inspired the actions. Here, one is not concerned as to whether, in fact, there was a fight. Instead the inquiry is why the supervisor took certain actions to investigate. Note that in this circumstance, the supervisor is the direct witness and can explain and be cross-examined on the question.

What constitutes hearsay? This can often pose sticky problems for advocates and arbitrators. Application of the somewhat stilted rule—"admitting it for the purpose of proving the truth of the matter asserted"—is often difficult in the heat of battle. A more workable, and generally accurate, test is to inquire whether the "sayer" can be cross-examined. The inability to do this and thus to better judge the reliability of the evidence is, after all, the essence of the hearsay problem.

Hearsay takes many forms. A letter from a disgruntled customer or, indeed, any written document may potentially constitute hearsay since the "testimony" comes from the document, not from its writer. Nevertheless, some documents are deemed sufficiently reliable to warrant admitting them, notwithstanding their hearsay nature. Remember, admission into evidence does not resolve the question of the weight to be attributed to any particular item—that truly is within the discretion of the neutral. The disputes turn on the more technical question of whether they should be admitted in the first place. One turns, then, to the various specific problems that seem to surface most regularly in the arbitration process.

Live Testimony

There is no admissibility problem with respect to live testimony in terms of its form, although objections might arise with respect to content. Testimony concerning offers of settlement, for example, is generally excluded on the grounds that it is irrelevant to the merits of the case and that admission would tend to stifle the desired goal of achieving compromise short of arbitration. However, an admission of guilt, for example, even in the context of a settlement offer, may well be admitted by the arbitrator.

Witnesses often make hearsay statements. When this happens, the result is that an absent witness "testifies" through

someone who heard him. The classic example is the one referred to earlier. Consider, however, the following examples:

(1) The witness testifies: "I heard John yell, 'I know where
you live and I'll get you after work.' "

Is this hearsay? The live witness is testifying that he *heard*
someone *say* "I know where you live, etc." However, assuming
this is a case where John is being disciplined for threatening
another employee, the statement is admissible. We are, after
all, not concerned with whether the statement itself is true, but
rather whether it was issued. We do not particularly care
whether John actually knows where the other employee lives or
whether it is *true* that he will "get him after work." We are in-
terested, instead, in whether the threat was issued. The live
witness, who heard the threat, is fully capable of testifying to
whether the comment was made, for he is a direct witness to
that. Opposing counsel is fully capable of cross-examining on
the question (How close was he to the employee? Was there
noise in the area? etc.). In general, the witness is able to contribute firsthand to the fact-finding process with respect to
whether the threat was made.

(2) The supervisor testifies: "I received a number of
continuing complaints from various employees about
this person."

Here again, it would be proper to admit the reports of complaints as in any way providing support for the purpose that
the complaints were true. The most that could be acknowledged, subject to cross-examination, is that complaints had
been received.

(3) The chief steward testifies that, at negotiations over a
particular contract section, the company said: "We
realize this may be ambiguous, but here is what we interpret this to mean. . . ."

In this case, the witness would have to testify that "he
heard the company. . . ." This is, of course, a secondhand account, but we must remember that what we are concerned
with is the statement itself as evidence of the company's intent.
It may be, of course, that this witness is not telling the truth;
the person who made the statement may conceivably deny it,

respond that it was taken out of context, etc. But it is the making of the statement itself that we are concerned with, and not its underlying truth.

Live testimony in arbitration is often subject to questions concerning relevance and materiality. Most arbitrators are loathe to impose strict constraints on these grounds, considering not only the therapeutic value of one's "having his say" but also the generally accepted approach, even in courts, that, absent a jury, one may well be less concerned about excluding potentially confusing or even prejudicial testimony.

Affidavits

An affidavit is a sworn statement by a witness and is generally proffered in lieu of live testimony. It is to be distinguished from a deposition, which is taken in the presence of opposing counsel who has had the opportunity to cross-examine the witness's statements.

The affidavit is clearly hearsay in nature and, moreover, subject to some questions of reliability inasmuch as (1) there is no opportunity for cross-examination and (2) the statement is often prepared in contemplation of the litigation.

There appears to be a split of authority as to whether affidavits are admissible at all, given their potentially suspect nature. At the least, the party offering such document must demonstrate unavailability of the declarant. This may arise as a result of a number of conditions, including death, mental incapacity, or even outright refusal to testify. If unavailability arises because the witness cannot be found, it is generally held that "due diligence" must be exercised in attempting to find him. When admitted, the weight to be attributed to such testimony may necessarily be decreased as a result of the inability to cross-examine.

Depositions

Depositions properly assume some greater weight in terms of their evidentiary impact, as a result of the witnesses having been subject to cross-examination. Moreover, they may be useful in terms of avoiding protracted hearings when the parties are satisfied to take evidence in the absence of the arbitrator and rely on the neutral's later review. Again, however, if there is a question as to admissibility, most arbitrators will require some demonstration of unavailability of the witness.

Personnel Records

Personnel records are documentary evidence submitted for the purpose of "testifying" to a certain event. For example, an employee's record may demonstrate that he or she was absent on a certain number of days, or that an employee had been suspended for five days at a certain time. This is secondhand evidence and an example of hearsay, from a technical standpoint. It is the document that is testifying to the questioned event. However, personnel records are normally considered as a "business records" exception to the hearsay rule. Thus, their reliability is assumed to be generally sound inasmuch as the records are prepared in the normal course of business, rather than drafted in contemplation of the arbitration hearing, and are usually maintained in a reasonably secure fashion so as to avoid unwarranted entries. There may be questions arising as to whether the purpose for which they are being submitted is appropriate, but the documents are generally admissible.

Pictures and Tapes

Photographs and tape recordings are another form of hearsay. They are secondhand evidence as to, for example, the layout of a plant or a conversation that occurred. But photographs may be admitted assuming a witness can testify that they are accurate representations of the area in question. Similarly, tapes must be demonstrated to be accurate recordings of the conversations that occurred. This is not to say that there may not be a battle over whether they are, in fact, accurate but only to say that, upon such finding, they may be admitted.

Doctor's Slips

A doctor's verification of illness or incapacity will frequently read:

Joe Jones was seen by me on May 3, 1982. He had a bad cold, and I told him to stay home for two days. Signed, T. Spina, MD

The doctor's slip is hearsay. (It is submitted for proving the truth of the assertion that Jones had a cold. Moreover, one cannot cross-examine the note to see if, in fact, Jones was ill.) Parties to the arbitration process often recognize the difficulty and expense of securing medical personnel as witnesses and these slips are often admitted and given weight. However, there should be no question that if the state of the witness's health is in serious question, such slips may fall well short of proving the case.

Transcripts of Testimony by a Witness in Former Proceedings

The transcript of testimony may be hearsay, if the purpose of the transcript is to fully substitute for the absent witness. If the testimony was under oath, there was opportunity to cross-examine on substantially the same issue, and the witness is presently unavailable, the evidence may be admitted.

Transcripts of prior testimony are often used for impeachment purposes. If, for example, Sam testifies at arbitration that he was home on a particular night, it is appropriate for opposing counsel to attempt to impeach that testimony by showing that Sam said, in another proceeding, that he had been somewhere else. Remember, we are not necessarily concerned with the truth of his earlier statement. What counts is that he said it at all and thereby made inconsistent statements.

Results of Other Proceedings

This is a controversial area. Generally, the question is whether the decision of a court, unemployment compensation tribunal, or other administrative agency on the same or related subject matters should be admitted for resolving a contested fact issue in the instant case. (This is to be distinguished from the impact of prior arbitration awards, to be considered below.) Many arbitrators appear willing to admit prior court determinations of guilt or innocence of, say, theft when an employee is being terminated for such theft. They reason that such determinations by judges or juries are matters of court record; that they are relevant elements of the moving party's case to show the validity of that party's position; that they may be meaningful in tipping the final scales; and that, in the case of conviction, they represent a finding against the grievant despite a potentially higher standard of proof than would be imposed in the arbitration proceeding.

The competing view is that the proceedings are separate and distinct; that the court involvement is between the state and the grievant; that the union and the employer were not involved as they are in the contract arbitration; and that to allow such evidence in at all, allegedly for "tipping the balance," is tantamount to relying on it entirely. In this case, the arbitrator would be improperly delegating his or her function—that of finding facts based on evidence adduced at the hearing—to another tribunal.

The least persuasive position is that the rulings of another body are simply "one more piece of evidence" that may eventually tip the scales. Without regard to the nature of the other hearing, the most that can be said is that another fact finder reached a particular conclusion on the same facts. But arbitration should not be a process of counting ballots. If the arbitrator is to take cognizance of the other finding, there should be a compelling reason. As indicated above, perhaps the arbitrator is persuaded that a guilty finding by a court is entitled to controlling weight. But from a practical standpoint, how does one handle the fact that the case may be on appeal? Should the arbitrator defer the decision pending the appeal? Should the arbitrator retain jurisdiction of the matter in the event the original decision is overturned? Should the parties agree to merely forego arbitration in any case where the matter is contested elsewhere? Or is this unnecessary because the arbitrator has done this for them?

Even those who object to the introduction of evidence of convictions recognize that guilty pleas or admissions made during the course of the hearings are admissible. If an admission has been made, it makes no difference in which forum this occurs. It is also true, however, that an individual may proceed to prove in the arbitration forum *why* the admission was made in court. It may have arisen as a plea bargain, out of ignorance of what pleading to the facts entailed, or on the advice of counsel to avoid the potentially damaging risks and costs of a full court trial.

There are also instances when a court conviction itself may be determinative of an arbitration case. If, for example, one of the conditions of employment is having a clear court record, as might be the case for a police officer or security guard, then any evidence of a court record of guilt as determined by a judge, jury, or admission would be received into evidence. In admitting such documentation, the standard is only the possession of a criminal record and not whether the employee was in fact guilty of the crime involved.

—— Case ——

In applying for a position as a cab driver, Rachel Annsack left blank the question, "Have you ever been convicted of a motor vehicle violation?" She was hired and drove her cab without incident for about three years. At that time, her boss, while talking to another cab company owner, learned she had worked for him 10 years earlier and had had her license suspended for one year for driving under the influence of alcohol. Her boss then terminated Rachel, giving rise to the instant arbitration.

Questions and Comments

(1) *How would you rule as arbitrator?*

The issue at hand is the falsification of the grievant's employment application. The employer has the right to inquire as to the prior performance and driving record of a potential employee to whom it is to entrust company equipment and passengers. To the extent the grievant denied the employer access to such vital information which is clearly a part of the record and relevant to her hiring, she secured her position under false pretenses. Although arbitrators tend to permit washouts of such infractions if the intervening record has been long and untarnished, it is unlikely that the three-year period will be held to overcome such a material omission and the termination would probably be upheld.

(2) *Would your answer be different if the evidence showed that the D.U.I. charge occurred prior to her initial cab-driving employment; that there was a one-year probationary period imposed; and that having completed the requisite extra driver training, she had been told by the court that her record was cleared?*

If the arbitrator found credible the grievant's assertion that she thought her criminal record had been wiped clean after the one-year period, then he might well excuse the omission. But otherwise, the arbitrator would probably find that it was the grievant's obligation to disclose the requested information, giving the employer the right to inquire or leaving her the opportunity to explain how the conviction arose. It is the denial of that opportunity for inquiry that would probably result in termination if the arbitrator felt that the grievant knew her court record was still extant.

Prior Arbitration Awards

Prior arbitration awards are often introduced at the hearing, and there has been a dearth of writings on the subject of the weight to be accorded them. It should be observed initially that, in most cases, these opinions do not constitute "evidence." Rather, they are a segment of the argument.

The question still remains; absent mutual agreement on the subject, what weight should be attributed them? Some parties, particularly in the context of an umpireship, consider prior awards absolutely binding. If a contract section has been previously interpreted, they reason, the arbitrator is clearly bound to employ that precise same interpretation.

Without such express guidance, this will normally not be the approach of an individual arbitrator. When the award being submitted is as a result of proceedings between the same parties under the same labor agreement, the chances are highest that the result will have some persuasive impact on the arbitrator. Commentators have suggested that most arbitrators will, under such circumstances, accept the holdings of the awards as binding, assuming the rationale is basically sound. This means they will follow the prior award even if they themselves might have rendered a different judgment. Arbitrators differ in this respect by matters of degree. Some neutrals place great weight on prior awards, treating them, in effect, as binding precedent in virtually all circumstances. Their theory is that, in submitting a matter to arbitration, the parties have agreed to seek an answer to a question of contract interpretation. Once that answer has been rendered, it becomes part of the agreement and may not be re-litigated. Should the answer be unsatisfactory, the parties must modify the agreement by negotiation. Thus, even if a prior award is completely contrary to any approach the arbitrator would have taken, those individuals will treat the matter as having been settled by the parties.

—— Case ——

The collective bargaining agreement between Hi-Sky Airlines and its ground personnel contains the following provisions:

Arbitration decisions under this Agreement shall be final, binding, and precedent-setting.

In 1965, the union grieved the airline's grooming policy (which had been incorporated into the labor agreement), contending it was unreasonable and arbitrary in several respects. An arbitrator ruled that the company was within its rights in enforcing the policy.

In 1982, the union grieved again, contending that times had changed and the same factors that led the arbitrator to reach the prior decision were no longer present. At arbitration, the company directed the arbitrator's attention to the above-quoted language. It maintained that the matter was not arbitrable, inasmuch as the prior award was "final, binding, and precedent-setting."

Question and Comment

(1) *What should the response be?*

That a prior award may control the outcome of a subsequent case does not mean that the case is not arbitrable. At the least, it is incumbent upon the new arbitrator to determine whether the facts of the case are sufficiently similar to the prior case as to warrant application of the earlier award. If the facts are "on all fours," the contract requires the conclusion that the case should come out the same way. But that is a conclusion on the merits and not on the question of arbitrability.

The argument concerning changing circumstances is intriguing in this respect, for while the question being asked is the same ("Is the grooming policy reasonable?"), the union seeks to distinguish the case on the premise that times have changed and that the standards applied in evaluating the policy must change as well. Unquestionably, there would be a diversity of opinion among arbitrators on this point.

3

External Law—Its Impact on the Labor Contract

When one considers external law in the context of arbitration, the image is of individual employees invoking statutory rights in addition to the rights provided them under the grievance and arbitration provisions of the parties' collective bargaining agreement. While that aspect of the external law problem as initiated in the context of conflicting rights under the National Labor Relations Act, and as subsequently evidenced by the decision of the U.S. Supreme Court in *Alexander v. Gardner-Denver*,[1] has its impact on the role of the arbitrator, there are a diversity of other "external law" questions with even more frequent and perhaps even greater impact which also deserve attention.

Beyond any constraints imposed by contract, an employer must conform to the prevailing laws of the jurisdiction in which it operates. Even absent a collective bargaining agreement, the employer is forced to conform to laws establishing minimum wages and maximum hours. In addition, the employer is required to abide by pertinent statutes and ordinances governing health, safety, security, and any other aspects of business operation that the local municipality, state, and federal governments determine to regulate or control.

The burden is on the employer to assure that it conforms to these ordinances, regulations, and statutes. That burden must

---

[1] 415 U.S. 36 (1974).

be borne whether or not the employees exercise their statutory rights to establish a union and engage in collective bargaining. If the parties negotiate a grievance and arbitration procedure, it may be the arbitrator's task, depending on the nature of the agreement, to interpret not only the contract but also the law.

Arbitrators and the Law

The relationship between arbitration and the judicial system has long been the subject of intense discussion. This discussion has focused, for the most part, on the inherent jurisdictional difficulties between private and public arbiters and has directed itself to the investigation and establishment of boundaries. The concern usually centers around the appropriate interplay between the labor contract and external law. However, the substantial increase in labor-related legislation combined with the Supreme Court's landmark 1974 decision in *Gardner-Denver* have created new, highly troublesome variations on the old theme. Incorporation of new legislation within collective bargaining agreements has created documents that inevitably assume a more public cast and that arguably may impose a quasi-public function upon the neutral arbitrator. These developments have, on occasion, raised substantial questions and some dire predictions as to the continuing viability of the present arbitral functions. It is appropriate, therefore, to consider the issue of the proper relationship between the private and public forums for dispute settlement.

There is no reason to question the basic and necessary premise that the job of an arbitrator is to interpret and apply the terms of the collective bargaining agreement. Surely that is the lesson of the *Steelworkers Trilogy*.[2] If it is not clear that the parties intended that external law resolve the matter, the arbitrator should assume they did not so intend.[3] If, however, the

---

[2] *United Steelworkers v. Enterprise Wheel & Car Corp.*, 363 U.S. 593 (1960); *United Steelworkers v. Warrior & Gulf Navigation Co.*, 363 U.S. 574 (1960); *United Steelworkers v. American Mfg. Co.*, 363 U.S. 564 (1960).

[3] The arbitrator "is not a public tribunal imposed upon the parties by superior authority which the parties are obliged to accept. He has no general charter to administer justice [for a community] which transcends the parties. He is rather part of a system of self-government created by and confined to the parties." Shulman, "Reason, Contract and Law in Labor Relations," 68 *Harv. L. Rev.* 999, 1016 (1955). See Feller, "The Coming End of Arbitration's Golden Age," in *Arbitration—1976*, Proceedings of the 29th Annual Meeting, National Academy of Arbitrators (Washington, D.C.: BNA Books, 1976), at 97.

parties have chosen to incorporate external law into their agreement, the arbitrator must interpret and apply that law.

The impact of external law upon the contract has been the subject of long and fervent debate.[4] One commentator has proposed that the collective bargaining agreement cannot be construed absent full consideration of external law.[5] His premise is that contracts in general are interpreted in accordance with all applicable laws. The approach is based on the assumption that the labor agreement is fully comparable to any other commercial contract. This proposal seemingly ignores the numerous problems of adapting traditional contract doctrines to the labor arena. As another commentator has persuasively argued, the collective agreement in the labor field is unique.[6]

The view as advocated by Professor Bernard Meltzer rejects the proposition that external law must always be consulted. Meltzer acknowledges that external law or public policy may be relevant when a broadly drawn contract provision clearly is formulated with an eye to incorporating public policy or when a contract clause is susceptible to two interpretations, one compatible with, the other repugnant to, an applicable statute. If, however, there is "an irrepressible conflict, the arbitrator ... should respect the agreement and ignore the law."[7]

The source of this debate is an ambiguity inherent in *United Steelworkers v. Enterprise Wheel & Car Corp.*[8] There, the Supreme Court suggested that an arbitrator is not confined to the text of a labor agreement and may in the appropriate case

---

[4]See Jones, "The Role of Arbitration in State and National Labor Policy," in *Arbitration and the Public Interest,* Proceedings of the 24th Annual Meeting, National Academy of Arbitrators (Washington, D.C.: BNA Books, 1971), at 42; Mittenthal, "The Role of Law in Arbitration," in *Developments in American and Foreign Arbitration,* Proceedings of the 21st Annual Meeting, National Academy of Arbitrators (Washington, D.C.: BNA Books, 1968), at 42; Morris, "Comment," in *Arbitration and the Public Interest, supra* at 65; Platt, "The Relationship Between Arbitration and Title VII of the Civil Rights Act of 1964," 3 *Ga. L. Rev.* 398 (1969); Sovern, "When Should Arbitration Follow Federal Law?" in *Arbitration and the Expanding Role of Neutrals,* Proceedings of the 23rd Annual Meeting, National Academy of Arbitrators (Washington, D.C.: BNA Books, 1970), at 29.

[5]Howlett, "The Arbitrator, the NLRB and the Courts," in *The Arbitrator, the NLRB, and the Courts,* Proceedings of the 20th Annual Meeting, National Academy of Arbitrators (Washington, D.C.: BNA Books, 1967), at 67, 83.

[6]Feller, "A General Theory of the Collective Bargaining Agreement," 61 *Cal. L. Rev.* 663, 720 (1973).

[7]Meltzer, "Rumination About Ideology, Law, and Labor Arbitration," in *The Arbitrator, the NLRB, and the Courts,* Proceedings of the 20th Annual Meeting, National Academy of Arbitrators (Washington, D.C.: BNA Books, 1967), at 16.

[8]363 U.S. 593 (1960).

look to the law for assistance in "determining the sense of the agreement." The Court, however, also demanded that an enforceable arbitration award "draw its essence from the collective bargaining agreement" and not from the requirements of external law. Notwithstanding the Court's otherwise strong endorsement of arbitration, this ambiguity bred a somewhat nebulous relationship between the arbitral and judicial processes.

In *Alexander v. Gardner-Denver Co.*, the Supreme Court held that an individual could proceed judicially to enforce his or her rights under Title VII of the Civil Rights Act of 1964 despite a final adverse decision in arbitration. The Court thereby added new substance to the debate on arbitral and judicial roles and brought arbitration to a new era. The Court did chart a reasonably clear course, at least in the context of Title VII, with respect to the arbitrator's function vis-à-vis external law. In providing for trial *de novo* in the courts, the Court assumed that the arbitrator would stick to the contract and abjure the law. In so doing, the Court adopted, *sub silentio*, Meltzer's view.

Significant questions remain after *Gardner-Denver*, for strict adherence to the contract does not resolve the problems raised by incorporation of external law into the contract. Thus, problems persist, not in cases involving an irrepressible conflict but in cases presenting no conflict at all, where the parties have specifically or impliedly chosen to incorporate external law into their agreement. There is no reason to disagree with the premise that when external law is so incorporated, the arbitrator may, indeed must, interpret and apply that law. This premise, however, does suggest a significantly expanded role for the arbitrator, the consequences of which are the subject of substantial debate.

Arbitration at a Crossroads

External law has had an increasing impact upon labor arbitration.[9] Professor David Feller therefore has concluded that

---

[9]E.g., Equal Pay Act of 1963, 29 U.S.C. §206 (1970); Occupational Safety and Health Act of 1970, 29 U.S.C. §§553, 651–678 (1970); Title VII of the Civil Rights Act of 1964, 42 U.S.C. §2000(e) (1970). See Aaron, "The Impact of Public Employment Grievance Settlement on the Labor Arbitration Process," in *The Future of Labor Arbitration in America* (Washington, D.C.: American Arbitration Association, 1976), at 1; Christensen, "Private Judges—Public Rights; The Role of Arbitration in the Enforcement of the National Labor Relations Act," in *The Future of Labor Arbitration in America, supra* at 113.

arbitration's future is dim because voyages by arbitrators into external law, outside their field of special expertise, will inevitably undermine arbitration in the eyes of the parties.[10] Concerning the arbitral role, Feller thinks the choice is between specialists, who possess expertise in labor relations and in the parties' internally formulated law, and generalists, who are devoid of special competence. He prefers the specialists—the arbitrator who serves a limited rather than an all-purpose function.

Feller thinks it unlikely that external rules will become familiar to the parties and to the arbitrators. Although Feller recognizes three potential responses to the problems generated by the increased legislative impact on labor agreements, he finds each response unsatisfactory. First, to the suggestion that arbitrators could decide all questions under both contractual and legal standards, Feller asserts that arbitrators may be incapable of performing this function. Another alternative lies in splitting litigation and developing a system of law in which the National Labor Relations Board or the courts would defer to arbitration as to contract issues but accept jurisdiction over remaining statutory questions, using the arbitration decision as datum not subject to review. This alternative, however, would be cumbersome and unworkable. Third, the NLRB could decide the external law question and also decide the meaning of the contract. The thought of the NLRB interpreting the contract causes Feller to shudder. Having found no satisfactory solution, Feller has concluded that, since the institution of arbitration must suffer one way or another, the best solution may be to have arbitrators construe external law in the interests of the parties.

Professor (now Judge) Harry Edwards objects to Feller's pessimism. Edwards agrees that the increasing interplay between public statutes and private contracts has presented a substantial challenge to arbitration. Edwards also thinks that the institution of arbitration will suffer to the extent it expands

---

[10]Feller, "The Impact of External Law Upon Labor Arbitration," in *The Future of Labor Arbitration in America, supra* note 9, at 83:

"[I]t remains, and will remain, enormously difficult to persuade the average court that the proper application and interpretation of an agreement is not a function which it is supremely competent to perform. Deference to arbitral competence was and is difficult to achieve. And I suggest it will be impossible to maintain if arbitrators extend themselves and regard arbitration as the tribunal in which broader policies than those contained in the agreements themselves are to be enforced."

beyond the traditional boundary defined by the "common law of the shop": "The more that arbitration and arbitrators look to decide 'legal' issues, the more the courts will be willing to overturn arbitral judgments. The more that the parties abandon informal, cheap and expeditious proceedings, the less likely it is that arbitration will be seen as a therapeutic [extension] of collective bargaining."[11] Yet Edwards rejects Feller's gloomy prognosis for the following reasons. First, the magnitude of the increase in external regulation of employment relations is not as significant as Feller would suggest. Second, the increase in public legislation has resulted in more, not fewer, disputes for arbitral resolution. Finally, it is entirely possible for arbitrators to deal with some, although not all, issues of public law.

The Feller-Edwards debate notwithstanding, the general concern is with arbitrators involving themselves in legal questions in such a way as to devitalize the public law through improper private administration and, in so doing, to diminish the importance of arbitration itself. Overall, both Edwards and Feller concern themselves with the existing structure of labor arbitration in light of radically changing legal realities. Feller concludes there is no acceptable alternative, thus foretelling the demise of the process. Edwards finds salvation in modifying existing grievance procedures.

Modifying the Arbitral Process

Edwards proposes a two-track system which will exclude the following grievances from arbitration: (1) those that allege only a breach of law; (2) those that charge both the union and the employer with discrimination; (3) those that seek a reformation of the contract; (4) those that claim inconsistency between the collective bargaining agreement and a court or administrative order; (5) those that sound in the nature of a class action; and (6) those that involve unsettled areas of law. Yet, even assuming that exclusion of these grievances is justifiable as a matter of good labor relations, it is unclear how one would implement the system. Who, for example, will decide that a

---

[11]Edwards, "Labor Arbitration at the Crossroads: The Common Law of the Shop v. External Law," 32 *Arb. J.* 65, 94 (1977).

matter involves an unsettled area of law or that a grievance alleges only a breach of law? The employer may well raise this claim, but often it will be unrealistic to expect the parties to have the necessary expertise to make an accurate assessment. Moreover, notwithstanding the contract language, unions confronted with the specter of fair representation suits cannot reasonably be expected to exclude the minority grievant on one of those grounds. It is more predictable that, should the charge fall within an excluded category, a cautious representative will assist the employee in amending the grievance.[12] Even if the claim does fall within one of Edwards' excluded categories, there may be a dispute on this point, which most probably will eventually be settled by an arbitrator.

Ideally, internal grievance machinery should be informal, speedy, inexpensive, and responsive to the particular problems of the work place. Yet, in the final analysis, Edwards' screening criteria merely add another, rather complex step to this process. Moreover, the bifurcated procedures will channel even more disputes to courts or administrative agencies. Thus, even if the system fulfills its expectations, there are substantial problems. Admittedly, there may be some virtue in avoiding multiple actions. At the same time, the two-track process may negate the possibility of conciliation, settlement, or even an arbitration award that might moot the cause of action in another forum.[13] In addition, by relegating discrimination disputes to the federal courts or agencies, the two-track system removes a significant aspect of industry-related disputes from the dispute settlement procedure. This hardly honors the tradi-

---

[12]Many grievances that allege discrimination also allege the standard contract violation. An individual disciplined for fighting in the plant, for example, may claim that the fighting was in self-defense and, moreover, that, as a result of race discrimination, discipline was unusually harsh. Inherent in the two-track system is the requirement that, should such an individual wish to process the grievance through standard channels, any reference to race discrimination should be excluded. This is easy enough—instead of claiming race discrimination, the grievant may simply claim disparate treatment and thereby jump back in the internal dispute settlement track. Nevertheless, assuming a major purpose of the two-track system is to obviate the problems posed by two bites at the apple, the system contains a very major loophole.

[13]In *EEOC v. McLean Trucking Co.*, 525 F.2d 1007 (6th Cir. 1975), the court held that a grievant who has succeeded at arbitration may not sue for additional benefits under Title VII. See *Williams v. General Foods Corp.*, 492 F.2d 399 (7th Cir. 1974); *Manning v. International Union*, 466 F.2d 812 (6th Cir. 1974); *Pearson v. Western Elec. Co.*, 13 FEP Cases 1200 (D. Kan. 1974). See also *Strozier v. General Motors Corp.*, 16 FEP Cases 363 (N.D. Ga. 1978), wherein a district court held that an employee who has accepted a "substantially equivalent" settlement in arbitration has waived the right to sue under Title VII.

tion of the *Steelworkers Trilogy*. Instead, the two tracks diminish the scope of the arbitration process and, in so doing, push arbitration toward the fate Feller has suggested.

Arbitration is the substitute for industrial strife or strikes, and parties must make every imaginable effort to keep the system procedurally simple. The requirements of due process and the difficult business of talking plainly to one another create a sufficiently arduous task. We need not complicate it further by the prospect of deciding which procedure goes with which grievant, thereby adding an additional level of potential dispute.

The basic problem in both the Feller and Edwards approaches, and in any two-track system in the labor-management context, is the assumption that the function of labor arbitrators must remain essentially static, notwithstanding the changing face of the agreements they are hired to interpret. A more realistic approach is to demand modifications by the arbitrators and the process which they assist in administering. If arbitration is to remain a viable force in the context of internal dispute settlement, arbitrators must be expected to deal with the expanded range of labor-related problems, including those encompassing legal concerns. What is required is an expanded concept of arbitral jurisdiction. Primarily, arbitration exists to serve the parties. Equally important is the perpetuation of the effective system of industrial self-government fashioned by companies and unions. It was the recognition of this system which, in large part, led the Supreme Court to endorse so extravagantly the concept of labor arbitration in the *Steelworkers Trilogy*.

Judge Edwards modified his views somewhat in 1982 when, addressing the National Academy of Arbitrators, he acknowledged that his experience as a judge had caused him to temper previous reservations about arbitrators deciding public law issues.[14] He endorsed the notion that there were many highly qualified arbitrators who could easily be trained

---

[14] See Edwards, "Arbitration of Employment Discrimination Cases: An Empirical Study," in *Arbitration—1975*, Proceedings of the 28th Annual Meeting, National Academy of Arbitrators (Washington, D.C.: BNA Books, 1976), at 59; Edwards, "Labor Arbitration at the Crossroads: The Common Law of the Shop v. External Law," 32 *Arb. J.* 65 (1977); Edwards, "Arbitration of Employment Discrimination Cases: A Proposal for Employer and Union Representatives," 27 *Labor L.J.* 265 (1976).

to deal with public law issues in the employment context, concluding that

> "As for the threat of public law issues being decided by private tribunals, I am now convinced that most public law issues inevitably find their way to the courts and, as a consequence, the courts invariably take the lead in the development of controlling legal standards with respect to such matters."[15]

There are additional reasons for parties to demand a more comprehensive response from the arbitrator. Admittedly, even the highly trained lawyer-arbitrator may have no more special expertise than would a court or administrative agency, at least with respect to interpretation and application of statutory and common law. Nevertheless, the arbitrator is in a better position to decide an issue that, albeit legal, is a product of the work place and is brought to the fore by virtue of the jointly administered grievance procedure. Assuming any breadth in fashioning a remedy, it is the arbitrator, not the courts or agencies, who is in the best position to fashion the most palatable solution, taking into consideration not simply law but also the industrial relationship to which the arbitrator brings a special brand of expertise.[16] Moreover, despite rising costs and time delays, it is still true that arbitration is significantly faster and cheaper for all parties than resort to the external forum.

Objections to a broader arbitral scope may be characterized as follows. First, it is alleged that arbitrators generally are not qualified to render decisions in legal matters and that arbitration systems normally do not employ discovery and other procedures essential to proper litigation of such questions. Second, it is claimed that matters of public law and policy should not be established by private arbitrators. These deficiencies, it is argued, will lead to increased judicial review and an ultimate diminution of judicial confidence in arbitration.

---

[15]Edwards, "Advantages of Arbitration Over Litigation: Reflections of a Judge," speech before the 35th annual meeting, National Academy of Arbitrators, May 28, 1982. See also Rubin, "Arbitration: Toward a Rebirth," in *Truth, Lie Detectors, and Other Problems in Labor Arbitration*, Proceedings of the 31st Annual Meeting, National Academy of Arbitrators (Washington, D.C.: BNA Books, 1979), at 30; Fletcher, "Arbitration of Title VII Claims: Some Judicial Perceptions," in *Arbitration Issues of the 1980s*, Proceedings of the 34th Annual Meeting, National Academy of Arbitrators (Washington, D.C.: BNA Books, 1982), at 218.

[16]See Newman, "Post-Gardner-Denver Developments in the Arbitration of Discrimination Claims," in *Arbitration—1975*, Proceedings of the 28th Annual Meeting, National Academy of Arbitrators (Washington, D.C.: BNA Books, 1976), at 36.

There is some merit to the initial point. An intriguing empirical study provides some grounds for skepticism as to arbitrators' capabilities in the Title VII area.[17] Of the 200 respondents to the questionnaire (all of them members of the National Academy of Arbitrators), only 52 percent said they read labor advance sheets on a regular basis. Fourteen percent indicated they felt competent to define the terms "bona fide occupational qualification," "reasonable accommodations/undue hardship," and "preferential treatment" and to explain thc current status of the law under Title VII with respect to each of these legal terms. Overall, only some 72 percent of the respondents felt competent to decide employment discrimination claims.

The sampling was small. In addition, one might quarrel with the premise of some of the questions. How many judges or attorneys could accurately define the current state of Title VII law without some degree of research? Intuitively, however, it is not too much to surmise that the majority of active labor arbitrators are not intimately familiar with either this or some of the other highly complex, relatively new, and rapidly changing areas of law.

It is not necessary to dismiss the possibility of arbitrators handling such matters in the context of a labor grievance. There are those in the profession who are supremely competent to handle such issues. Because it is the appropriate burden of the parties to administer the contract, it is incumbent upon them to select the arbitrator with care, inquiring if necessary in advance to determine his or her sphere of competence and thus proceeding perhaps more carefully than in the normal selection procedure. This is no more than a cautious party does in seeking legal counsel in any context.

The objection is also made that, regardless of their expertise, arbitrators should not take on public law issues. Feller thinks such arbitral involvement will lead to the inevitable demise of the entire system. Edwards agrees that arbitrators should stay away from the law, but for different reasons. Edwards is concerned that (1) arbitrators may be wrong, and (2) their errors, if honored by a public tribunal through deference

---

[17]Edwards, "Arbitration of Employment Discrimination Cases: An Empirical Study," in *Arbitration—1975*, Proceedings of the 28th Annual Meeting, National Academy of Arbitrators (Washington, D.C.: BNA Books, 1976), at 59.

to arbitration, may distort the development of precedent. Errors will, of course, occur, and it may be that deferral will result in the apparent sanctioning of an untoward result. To a certain extent, these problems can be met by the parties' careful selection of competent neutrals and the courts' cautious exercise of their deferral discretion. There is, however, no need to dispute the proposition that arbitrators should not be defining or otherwise promulgating public law. They simply are not doing so. Arbitration awards are not systematically reported or cross-indexed in a fashion which would lead to even a potentially consistent body of precedent. Arbitration is and always has been a private affair.[18] That the parties have incorporated certain statutes within their agreement does not make it less private, particularly with *Gardner-Denver's* affirmation that such incorporation will not deprive the courts of plenary jurisdiction.

To avoid potential derogation of statutory rights, it is incumbent upon federal courts to maintain vigilance with respect to individual rights and to be consistently willing to review the merits of arbitration cases involving such rights. Only in this manner may one ensure against de facto infringement on public rights by private processes. This rather broad review would constitute greater judicial involvement with arbitral proceedings than arbitrators or parties have traditionally expected or desired. Considering, however, that external law is more of a factor than ever before, this is to be welcomed as well as expected. While one may have justifiable qualms concerning a court's intervention in contractual matters that previously were handled by arbitrators, there is no reason to conclude that exercise of judicial jurisdiction over the legal questions necessarily will lead to the demise of arbitration or abandonment of the principles of the *Steelworkers Trilogy.*

Express Incorporation of the Law

In some contracts, parties negotiate provisions stating that the contract is to be interpreted and applied in a manner

---

[18]But see Summers, "Labor Arbitration: A Private Process with a Public Function," 34 *Rev. Jur. U.P.R.* 477 (1965).

consistent with external law, i.e., incorporating external law by reference. In such situations the arbitrator is presumably obliged to adhere to the contract requirement of compliance with the external law as he would be bound by any other contract provision, even in cases where the parties do not raise it, or even if they argue it inexpertly or wrongly. Some arbitrators undertake their own investigation of the legal citations, but most will rule only on what is presented to them, acknowledging, perhaps, the inadequacy and potential lack of finality in their so doing. Some will decline to take on the external law issue, confining their decision to rulings on other portions of the contract and leaving the parties to challenge any ruling which they feel is contrary to that external law.

In many contracts incorporating external law by reference, the problem is compounded by vague or even contradictory standards. Take the following provision:

> This Contract shall be applied consistent with applicable federal, state, and local laws.

The arbitrator's task of interpreting the contract may be easiest if the external law is ignored. But even with the contractual requirement of adherence to external law, such a mandate may cause no difficulty if the law is consistent with the contractually derived result. It is where there is disparity that the difficulty arises. Arbitrators are, of course, anxious to avoid placing the parties in a posture which will force them into litigation over the alleged illegality of an award, or the impropriety of an award in which the arbitrator deliberately ignores the mandate of consistency with external law. When that "external law" is manifest in a decision of the U.S. Supreme Court establishing the final and binding law of the land, conformity thereto is logically attainable. But where there is no such ruling, where several circuits of the judiciary are at odds, where the federal and state courts or statutes differ, or where there is an administrative ruling or local ordinance which runs against the arbitrator's inclinations under the contract or against his understanding of the weight of the law, the problems intensify. They are, as suggested above, often exacerbated by the lack of adequate input from the parties' spokespersons as to what indeed the external law requires of the arbitrator. Unless the parties are both represented by experienced attorneys who are well versed in all aspects of the external law issue, the arbitrator may be deprived of the input necessary for him to properly weigh and determine the external law issue. Less than adequate presentations on the external law—or worse, disparate presentations or a presentation on the external law issue by one side and silence by the other side—raise the risk that such considerations will not be adequately presented to the arbitrator. The consequences may be an evaluation and/or application of that external law which is inadequate or inaccurate, increasing the potential for subsequent judicial review and reversal.

Public Sector Ramifications

The problems of external law are amplified when one considers arbitration in the public sector. There, any uncertainty as to whether the employer is authorized to negotiate a contract at variance with the law is moot. The parties' agreement is between the union and the government; one must assume conformity to, and compliance with, the prevailing law. Even though the law may not be specifically incorporated by reference in the contract, it is an omnipresent force which is ignored only at the peril of the parties. Indeed, the prevailing law has such an impact on public sector agreements that conformity thereto becomes in effect a condition of employment, thus binding on the arbitrator as well as the parties.

Federal Sector

No area of external law is as pervasive in its impact on the arbitrator as is federal law in federal sector labor agreements. The existence of the collective bargaining agreement and the right to arbitrate are dependent upon the option of the federal employer, as initially set forth in federal executive orders from President Kennedy forward and more recently embodied in legislation creating the Federal Labor Relations Authority. Any contractual context in which the arbitrator might seek to rule is therefore governed by the acts of the federal government creating the contract and governing its interpretation and application. Arbitrators who apply the traditional private sector standards do so at some risk, but here, too, there is too frequently woefully inadequate presentation of the issues (contractual as well as external law issues). The high incidence of review of arbitral decisions, the complexity of the controlling external rules and regulations governing the proceedings, and the very collective bargaining agreement impose a significant burden on the arbitrator to know, to question, and, at least, to be receptive to the relevant external law, rules, and regulations.

For example, in the private sector, awarding attorney's fees to a prevailing party is virtually unheard of. But in the federal sector, the Back Pay Act, 5 U.S.C. §5596(b)(1), authorizes the award of attorneys' fees under certain circumstances, in accordance with standards established under the Civil Service Reform Act, 5 U.S.C. §7701(q).

The burgeoning incidence of federal sector grievance arbitration requires that more and more arbitrators be called upon to resolve these issues. The federal sector may prove to be, after all the requisite, careful footwork, the prime arena for the training of a new generation of arbitrators.

——— **Case** ———

The administration of a federal agency has a regulation providing that the local director shall make case load assignments. The parties' agreement contains the following provision:

PRECEDENCE OF LAWS AND REGULATIONS

In the administration of all matters covered by this Agreement, officials and employees are governed by existing or future laws and regulations of appropriate authorities, other published agency policies and regulations in existence at the time this Agreement was approved, and by subsequently published agency policies and regulations required by law or by the regulations of appropriate authorities.

When the local director increased the case load of employees pursuant to a directive from Washington, the employees filed a grievance, alleging viola-

tion of the work load clause of the agreement, reading
as follows:

> The employer will refrain from imposing an un-
> manageable case load for employees. The par-
> ties recognize that the number of cases each indi-
> vidual employee can manage is dependent on
> many factors, such as geographic area covered,
> type of case, grade level of case, priority pro-
> grams, and other assigned duties.

In answering the grievance, the agency noted
that the *Federal Register* grants the employer the
right to assign work. This, it argued, gives the
employer the authority to determine whether a work
load is unmanageable, and that such management
prerogatives were not negotiable. It urges that the
grievance be dismissed as not being arbitrable.

Question and Comment

(1) *As arbitrator, how would you rule?*

The crux of the parties' dispute is whether the management rights clause or the work load clause of the parties'
agreement controls on the issue of management's right to
assign and judge work loads. There is no prohibition against
the arbitrator interpreting or applying the disputed sections,
and it becomes incumbent upon the arbitrator to resolve the
dispute as to whether the contract grants to the employer the
substantive right it asserts. Accordingly, most arbitrators
would probably find the dispute arbitrable.

On the merits, the issue is whether the employer can re-
serve to itself the right to assess whether the work loads are
unmanageable. The parties did agree that administration of
the contract would be conducted in conformity with the external law, in this case contained in the *Federal Register* providing the right to set work loads. Presumably the *Federal Register*
mandate permits the establishment of unmanageable as well
as manageable work loads. But since the work load clause of
the parties' agreement contains negotiated language prohibit-

ing an unmanageable case load, and since the employer agreed
to that language without the stipulation that it was to define
"unmanageable" or retain jurisdiction over such definition, it
must follow that the parties agreed to an objective test of "unmanageable" case loads and that the mutual dispute settlement machinery they agreed to is the appropriate process for
assessing whether, indeed, work loads are manageable. The
arbitrator should then proceed to assess whether the employer
violated the work load clause by its assignments.

——— Case ———

Federal law prohibits employees from striking,
and those who do are to be terminated and barred
from federal employment for three years. Employees
in one facility of a federal agency engage in a con-
certed refusal to work on the day their collective
bargaining agreement expires, and before agreement
is reached on a new contract. Of the 4000 who remain out of work, the employer terminates only the
150 who were observed on the picket line during the
time they were scheduled to be at work. The remaining 3850 were issued penalties from written warnings up to 10-day suspensions. The parties' agreement contains no language referring to the "external
law." The terminated employees grieve the action
and appeal to arbitration.

Questions and Comments

(1) *If you were the employer, how would you argue?*

The employer would argue that this contract, like any in
the federal sector, was negotiated and must be administered
and interpreted by the arbitrator in light of the existing law
against federal employees striking; that the strike ban requires
termination of those striking; and that regardless of the fact
that lesser or no penalties were imposed upon the remaining
3850 employees, the arbitrator is forced to order the termination of the 150 grievants.

(2) *If you were the union, how would you argue?*

The union would argue that the contract contains no language requiring the termination of strikers; that the employer waived the right to invoke the statute by failing to terminate all 4000 strikers; and that the disparate treatment and condonation of the strike activity of 3850 justify a similar suspension penalty for the grievants. Finally, it would be argued that the action of the pickets was an exercise of their constitutional right of free assembly and freedom of speech, was protected activity under the NLRA, and was, in any event, not deserving of such a heavy penalty.

(3) *As arbitrator, how would you rule?*

This case presents the arbitrator with a substantial dilemma. On the one hand, federal law clearly requires termination of strikers. If the law is incorporated by reference in the agreement, it may hardly be ignored. Even without specific language, an arbitrator might conclude that the strike ban pre-existed the parties' agreement, was well known in the federal sector, and, indeed, created a working condition under the parties' agreement which, when breached, justified imposition of the discharge. On the other hand, to so rule would be to ignore the apparent condonation of strike activity by the majority of the employees. The arbitrator might well attempt to distinguish the 150 grievants from among the 4000 who declined to work on the theory that the picketing action was more than a mere absenting from work—that it constituted evidence of strike leadership or at least an active role in discouraging other employees from reporting to work. This dilemma might also lead the arbitrator to base the decision purely on the contract, finding that the picketing activity constituted just cause for discharge under the circumstances, while it was within management's discretion to impose lesser sanctions or none at all on the remaining employees. In any event, given the federal ban on strikes, it is unlikely that the picketing would be endorsed as a legitimate exercise of a private or public right.

Prospects for the Future

The fear among arbitrators following the *Gardner-Denver* decision was that the finality of arbitration awards would become a thing of the past, with the arbitration step but a prelude (and a legalistic procedure, at that) to court litigation; that the parties' faith in the process and its finality would be shattered; and that the institutional value of arbitration as the parties' jointly developed conflict resolution process would fast erode as the judicial review ground swell grew, marking the end of an era.

This chamber of horrors has not materialized. Cases involving challenge to arbitral awards because of alleged disregard or violation of individual statutory rights have, in fact, been few and far between. Such statutory rights cases are being pursued but their processing does not seem to have had any appreciable impact on the traditional labor-management grievances and arbitration procedure.

Thus, although the arbitration community has been alerted to the prospects of disruption to its tradition as a private, final, and binding dispute settlement forum, the ramifications of such potential disruption appear to have been minimal. The practice of arbitration continues with its main, albeit not exclusive, focus on the collective bargaining agreement. Arbitrators can scarcely be viewed as fulfilling the parties' expectations of resolving disputes if they stolidly ignore the realities of potential judicial review with its prospects of destroying the finality of such awards.

The history of arbitration and the external law shows that arbitrators ignore the external law at their own (and the parties') peril; that they should be aware of potential concerns in the area of external law; that they should seek to accommodate thereto as long as it does no disservice to their primary responsibilities under the contract; and that parties' spokespersons should be particularly alert to the pendency of external law quesions so that when related cases are heard in arbitration, they will be brought within the ambit of the arbitrator's role in resolving such contractual disputes. Working together, arbitrators and advocates may thus have greater sensitivity to the external law questions and, recognizing them, proceed with arbitration in a manner that resolves rather than exacerbates the parties' pending problems.

Too great a concern for external law issues will vitiate any need for arbitration or, at best, turn arbitration into a pre-court proceeding. Too little concern ducks an issue that is vital to the parties and, indeed, vital to arbitration as a means of resolving the parties' disputes. In treading the middle ground, it is hoped that arbitrators will provide the final and binding judgments on which the parties have come to rely.

Let us turn to an examination of some legal concerns other than the statutory enactments referred to above that do have an impact on the arbitration process.

Constitutional Rights

Arbitrators are frequently confronted with claims that certain employment activities are protected by the U.S. Constitution's Bill of Rights. Thus, an employee who produces scurrilous anti-employer diatribe and circulates it to friends throughout the plant, or prints and distributes it as people walk out the plant gate, can be heard to claim during his discharge arbitration that such activity is protected as an exercise of freedom of speech or freedom of the press. Likewise, an employee stopped for a routine search of his lunch box and discovered with stolen products on leaving the plant can be heard to invoke at his termination hearing the constitutional prohibition against unreasonable search and seizure.

In hearing such cases, arbitrators will frequently recognize that there are such constitutional protections but that the exercise thereof may be at the expense of the individual's employment; that there is no constitutional right to one's job; and that the employer in the exercise of its managerial authority may establish certain reasonable rules and discipline for violation of these rules. Among such reasonable rules would logically be a ban against defaming or sabotaging the company's image among the public or its own employees; a ban against removing products from the plant or refusing to have one's locker or lunch box searched; or a ban against bringing a handgun or other dangerous weapon into a tranquil office setting.

Employees' claims for religious exemptions from certain practices occasionally raise more troublesome questions.

—— **Case** ——

Jonathan Samuel is an Orthodox Jew whose religious tenets bar him from working on Saturdays. This had never been a problem at his job until increasing work loads led the employer to invoke its contractual right to require Saturday overtime work. Samuel refused, was disciplined, continued to refuse, and was ultimately discharged. He grieved and appealed the case to arbitration.

Questions and Comments

(1) *As arbitrator, how would you rule?*

Most arbitrators would find that the employer's right to require overtime was contractually justified and that the employee, regardless of his religious convictions, was required to conform to the contractual obligation to make himself available for the appropriate share of the Saturday work. They would probably note that the grievant held his job conditionally upon the commitment to conform to the requirements of the contract and that his exercise of his freedom of religion did not justify an arbitrator's rewriting of the contract to provide a Saturday work exception for religious Jews. If Samuel wants to exercise his religious belief against work, the appropriate recourse would be to find alternative employment someplace where Saturday work is not required. His termination would probably be sustained.

(2) *Would your answer differ if the overtime was voluntary, but the grievant was evading his share of such Saturday work?*

Most arbitrators would respect Samuel's right to decline Saturday overtime work if such work were voluntary at the time of his employ. Even though his rejection of Saturday overtime work created a disparate distribution of overtime, they would be likely to find that his refusal was reasonable in light of his religious convictions, and permit his refusal without penalty. A different result would probably obtain, however, if, after some years of his employ, the parties negotiated a mandatory overtime provision. As a member of the bargaining unit, he would be bound by the revised contract provision and be required to serve the overtime even if it had been voluntary when he was first hired.

(3) *What if Samuel were a member of a 200-member, self-proclaimed religious cult that would not work on Wednesday nights?*

The thrust of the earlier answers was that an employee could invoke his religious bar to overtime work if the work system permitted such voluntary refusals, but that he would be required to work or leave his employment if the overtime requirement was mandatory. Thus, the legitimacy of the religious claim or authenticity of the religious affiliation would not enter into the case as it might if the cult member employee were seeking to invoke religious days off under a contract.

Note that there are situations where federal law might require that the employer "accommodate" religious views under certain circumstances. Nevertheless, the arbitrator who is of the (majority) school that the labor agreement controls, in terms of his or her assignment, will resolve these cases in the manner suggested above.

Due Process

Private sector arbitration is essentially a private matter.[19] Nevertheless, parties have adopted many procedural protections in the context of the arbitration process.

------

[19]But see *Holodnak v. Avco Corp.*, 381 F. Supp. 191 (D. Conn. 1974), modified, 514 F.2d 285 (2d Cir. 1975), wherein the court suggested that a heavy mix of federal contracts might require the conclusion that constitutional due process guarantees should be inferred in the grievance process.

An employee accused of theft may decline to testify at his arbitration hearing for a variety of reasons. The Fifth Amendment guarantee against self-incrimination is directed to criminal proceedings and is thus inapplicable in this private, contractual matter. Whether the arbitrator will draw a negative inference from the refusal to testify will, therefore, depend upon a number of elements. At the outset, even without a constitutional analysis, one may properly expect the employer to prove the case. It is not the employee's burden to prove his or her innocence. If the employer has failed to sustain a prima facie case, the employee should prevail, even without testimony or evidence being presented. But if a basic case has been made, an arbitrator may well draw a negative inference from the refusal of an individual to deny or refute the charges.

A different light would be shed on the grievant's failure to testify, however, if there were a pending criminal investigation against him. In such a case, the arbitrator might be less likely to expect rebuttal of the charges in deference to the individual's desire to remain silent pending the forthcoming criminal matter.

Although arbitration has endeavored to remain aloof from the strict legalistic procedures of the courts, it has throughout its growth respected certain basic legal rights which have, one might conclude, contributed appreciably to its acceptability. Even though invoked and relied on by laymen rather than lawyers, the parties have come to respect and accept such rulings as a necessary protection in their contract-based system.

Arbitration and External Agencies

The discharge of an employee may be a violation of the "just cause" section of a labor agreement. It may also violate Section 8(a)(3) of the National Labor Relations Act, which prohibits discrimination for anti-union reasons. Similarly, a unilateral reduction in wages may violate a number of contractual requirements, including those establishing wages, and the "recognition section," wherein the employer acknowledges the union as the elected representative of employees for bargaining purposes. But that action might also constitute a violation of the duty to bargain under Section 8(a)(5) of the NLRA.

Other agencies, too, might have a direct interest in what are otherwise company-union matters. An employee disciplined for refusing to do a job she believes is inherently unsafe may have a contract claim, but may also invoke provisions of the Occupational Safety and Health Act. How does one accommodate these potentially conflicting decisions of different bodies? Is it the decisions of the arbitrator or the administrative bodies that should eventually prevail and, from a procedural standpoint, how does one avoid double hearings on every issue?

In 1964, the U.S. Supreme Court directed itself to the question of conflict between the arbitrators and the National Labor Relations Board.[20] The Court recognized that, as a practical matter, arbitration might end the controversy and that it, like collective bargaining, helped to promote the statutory objective of industrial peace. Recognizing that the NLRB would generally defer to an arbitration award (see the discussion of the *Spielberg* case, below) assuming the award was fair and that the results were not repugnant to the Act, the Court addressed the question of who had the final say:

> "Should the Board disagree with the arbiter, . . . the Board's ruling would, of course, take precedence; and if the employer's action had been in accord with that ruling, it would not be liable for damages under Section 301 [of the National Labor Relations Act]."[21]

The concept of deferring to an arbitration award was first examined by the Board in *Spielberg Manufacturing Company*.[22] After an arbitrator sustained the company's refusal to reinstate four strikers, charges were filed against the employer under the National Labor Relations Act. The Board deferred to the arbitrator, noting that

> "the proceedings appear to have been fair and regular, all parties had agreed to be bound, and the decision of the arbitration panel is not clearly repugnant to the purposes and policies of the Act. In these circumstances we believe that the desirable objective of encouraging the voluntary settlement of labor disputes

---

[20]*Carey v. Westinghouse Elec. Corp.*, 375 U.S. 261 (1964). *Carey* was a case involving representational issues. The Supreme Court has also approved the Board's policy deferring to arbitration where unfair labor practice issues were involved. See *NLRB v. C&C Plywood Corp.*, 385 U.S. 421 (1967).

[21]*Carey v. Westinghouse Elec. Corp.*, 375 U.S. at 272.

[22]112 NLRB 1080, 36 LRRM 1152 (1955).

will be best served by our recognition of the arbitrator's award."[23]

Note that the Board's deferral in the above-noted situations arose after an arbitration award had been rendered. Prior to 1971, however, the Board generally would accept cases that had not been arbitrated, even though arbitration machinery was available. Then, in 1971, the Board issued its decision in *Collyer Insulated Wire*.[24] There, the employer was charged under Section 8(a)(5) of the Act with unilaterally changing working conditions during the contract term. It increased the wage rate for certain employees, among other things. Before an NLRB trial examiner, it was contended that the changes were in accordance with the contract as well as congruent with past practice. The trial examiner decided the case, but the Board concluded this was erroneous. The dispute, it held, was essentially over the interpretation of the collective bargaining agreement, and therefore should have been resolved pursuant to the grievance procedure and arbitration. Accordingly, it held, the complaints should have been dismissed. The Board retained jurisdiction to insure that the dispute was either settled or properly submitted to arbitration and that the arbitration procedures would be in accordance with the *Spielberg* requirements. The Board set forth a number of criteria for such pre-arbitration deferral:

(1) availability of arbitration;
(2) likelihood that the award of an arbitrator will be honored;
(3) a "sufficient identity" between the contract issue before the arbitrator and the statutory issue before the Board.

Two members of the NLRB dissented in *Collyer* and, while the doctrine has been applied in most cases, there is some indication that the Board will not defer in cases involving union discrimination charges.

---

[23] *Id.* at 1153.
[24] 192 NLRB 837, 77 LRRM 1931 (1971).

Deferrals to Administrative Agencies by Arbitrators

There are occasions when the rulings of administrative agencies on the same issue are submitted for the arbitrator's consideration. Arbitrators vary in their responses. However, inasmuch as the arbitrator's first responsibility is to application and interpretation of the collective bargaining agreement, it may be argued that such external decisions should be excluded from his or her consideration. Thus, for example, the decision of an unemployment compensation panel on the question of the propriety of a grievant's discharge or, for that matter, the decision of a court where the offending conduct was also criminal in nature should be disregarded, assuming the arbitrator's function is to find facts and render a judgment. Some arbitrators accept these external conclusions "for what they are worth." But the difficult—indeed, unanswerable—question is "what *are* they worth?" Is a criminal conviction entitled to more weight than an acquittal, since it was made on the basis of "beyond all reasonable doubt"? What happens to the arbitration award if the criminal conviction is reversed on appeal? These questions have led many arbitrators to simply reject all external rulings and decide the case on the basis of the evidence before them. This is surely more in keeping with the well-accepted premise that the arbitrator is bound to interpretation and application of the collective bargaining agreement.

The Contract Provisions

4

Management Rights

Reserved Rights

Prior to collective bargaining, the only restrictions imposed on managerial authority were those emanating from statutes such as minimum wage and maximum hour laws. It stands to reason that the advent of collective bargaining would result in an effort by unions to modify those previously exclusive prerogatives. It is not unionization itself or even the requirement of collective bargaining that results in the employer's surrender of its previously comprehensive authority. Rather, it is the employer's effort to seek agreement that leads to voluntary surrender of certain managerial rights.

Through the process of collective bargaining, the union seeks to secure improved benefits to be codified in the parties' agreement. To the extent the union is successful in its efforts to accomplish such things as improvement of wages and holidays, and reduction of hours of work and mandatory overtime assignments, the company agrees to surrender its control over such matters and to specify in the labor agreement how much of that authority it is willing to surrender.

To the extent the parties specifically agree to certain employee benefits, the contract seeks to set standards of operation for the life of the agreement. Those various clauses—and the problems of interpretation and application that flow from them in the months and years following their negotiation—are the thrust of most of this volume. But there are a multitude of subjects that, while potentially ripe for specific consideration in the parties' agreement, are not incorporated and that, indeed, do not even come up for discussion during negotiations.

The question arises as to where the authority resides over those matters not specifically negotiated by the parties. One view holds that prior to collective bargaining there is a *tabula rasa*, with neither the employer nor the union possessing any non-negotiated rights. Arthur Goldberg, then counsel for the United Steelworkers of America, described it in 1956 as follows:

> "The union has the right to pursue its role of representing the interest of the employee with the same stature accorded it as is accorded management."[1]

The more prevalent view is that those rights not specifically negotiated away from management by the union remain unfettered and within the control of the employer. This view is termed the "residual" or "reserved rights" theory and endorses the employer's right to operate the enterprise in the same manner as prior to collective bargaining, except as restricted by the language of the negotiated contract provision. Therefore, the employer is deemed to have retained those rights not contracted away and the burden is on the union to establish that a management right has been surrendered rather than upon the employer to spell out such retained rights in the contract, or otherwise prove that they have been retained. The significance of this is that the employer need not take the initiative in identifying rights in the contract language. The employer's reserved or retained rights are considered to exist even though the employer does not insist on listing them in the collective bargaining agreement.

Rights associated with determining the product, price, methods of operation, hiring and supervision of personnel, and rule making are matters uniquely within the province of the employer and rarely subject to negotiation. These and related matters are inherent managerial rights that accrue to the employer whether or not specified in the agreement. An employer may decline to spell out its managerial rights in a contract for

---

[1] Arthur Goldberg, "Management's Reserved Rights: A Labor View," in *Management Rights and the Arbitration Process*, Proceedings of the 9th Annual Meeting, National Academy of Arbitrators (Washington, D.C.: BNA Books, 1956), at 121.

fear that securing the union's acquiescence to them might be viewed by arbitrators as an implication that the company was unable to secure agreement, or did not even assert its rights to the others, thus barring it from asserting any other, nonenumerated rights.

Negotiated Management Rights Clause

To make clear to the union that the employer is retaining its unsurrendered rights, and to forestall disputes that may arise over silence on a particular topic, employers usually secure union acquiescence to certain managerial language in the parties' agreement. A management rights clause may strengthen the company's claim that it possesses a certain authority, but the absence of such a clause will not, itself, force the conclusion that such authority is lacking. Such language may be in the form of a blanket retention, such as:

Management retains all rights except as otherwise provided in this agreement.

Or the agreement may contain more specific language, such as:

Management retains all rights except as otherwise provided, including but not limited to the right to

1. manage and direct the work force,
2. determine the method and manner of operation,
3. hire, promote, assign, transfer, discipline, lay off, discharge, and otherwise direct employees, and
4. otherwise utilize its personnel and facilities to achieve the most efficient operation of the plant.

Indeed, the detailed enumeration of specifically reserved management rights may fill a page or two of the collective bargaining agreement.

The extent to which employees' rights are successfully carved from the original block of management prerogatives varies with the issue, the contract language, and perhaps the intent of the parties as reflected in their negotiating history. To the extent there may be a difference of opinion on the issue, it may also be subject to interpretation by an arbitrator.

In some areas, the union has a strong burden of showing that it extracted certain specified rights from the employer. In other cases, the specific right, although not listed in the contract, may be reasonably implied from the grant of more general rights such as seniority, the union recognition clause, or, indeed, the grievance procedure itself.

────── **Case** ──────

During negotiations of the parties' first agreement, they agreed to the following management rights clause:

> The company shall have the unfettered right to discipline and discharge employees.

In negotiating the second agreement, the company agreed to the union's proposal for a grievance and arbitration clause defining a grievance as "any dispute as to the interpretation or application of this Agreement." The previous language was retained. At the hearing, the union spokesperson argues that the new language was designed to subject improper disciplinary actions to challenge through the grievance procedure, that such is the universal impact of the provision, that it thus altered the prior unilateral authority of the employer, and that it was incumbent upon the employer to state that it felt to the contrary.

The company argues that its "unfettered" right to discipline and discharge was unaltered and unaffected by the second negotiations, that the new provision was restricted by the management rights clause, and that it was incumbent on the union to amend the management rights clause if it wished to establish neutral review under just cause standards.

Questions and Comments

(1) *If you were the arbitrator, how would you decide?*

There are two substantial—and contradictory—arguments that could be raised here. The first is as follows: The preexisting language of the management rights clause clearly established an "unfettered" right to discipline or discharge. To the extent the subsequent negotiations were intended to impose a restriction on that broad right, it was necessary that the restriction be explicitly set forth either in the form of a revision of the management rights clause or a clear statement in the grievance and arbitration clause that it was intended to apply to discipline and discharge. If there was a contradiction in language between the first and second agreements, it might be held that the explicit right of the later agreement would control. But in the absence of clear language or clear intent, it should be held that the prior language continued in effect, with the new language applying to matters other than those in which the employer had specifically retained its unilateral authority.

The other argument would contend that the new language is contradictory, specific, and, hence, controlling. The parties know how to incorporate restrictions on the subject matter of grievances, it would be argued, and they clearly incorporated no such language here. To the contrary, they eliminated the restrictions. Under these circumstances, this latter argument would probably prevail.

(2) *Assume the original clause had not been replaced. If the union had said in negotiations that it intended the new clause to supersede the management rights clause, how would one view the employer's silence in response?*

Some arbitrators might hold the company was obligated to respond that it did not agree with that view and that the company's silence constituted acquiescence to the union's statement. But the language is still in the agreement. The conclusion would be that the employer's prior language was still in effect and that such a one-sided assertion would not be sufficient to overcome the clear language of the management rights clause.

There may be instances where a certain item normally considered a managerial prerogative (level of staffing, for example) has traditionally been bargained. If there is a history of negotiating the inclusion or exclusion of what would otherwise be a specific right, that negotiating history might be determinative of whether or not a management right had been negotiated away. In this respect, careful, detailed notes of negotiating sessions may prove helpful either in proving the party's case or in persuading the leadership that it may be more prudent to resolve the dispute prior to arbitration.

Facing a midnight strike deadline, negotiators often agree upon contract language that obfuscates rather than clarifies. While each party had a clear understanding of what its side wanted and therefore an understanding of what its side thought the agreed-upon language meant, there may nevertheless be no meeting of the minds. Moreover, in too many cases the parties have a tacit understanding that the agreed-upon language does not really solve a particular problem, but the lateness of the hour and the pressure of more important "strike" issues make it palatable. The assumption may be that neither party has surrendered its objectives on that point. In any event, one party may say to itself or even to the other team's representatives that the issue probably will not arise again during the life of this agreement, and if it does, it can always be clarified by an arbitrator. The risk of such a course is obvious. But the realities of last-minute bargaining will, no doubt, continue to prevail and to provide more work for the neutrals.

Disputes Over Management's Authority to Determine the Method of Operations

There is seldom any union challenge to the theoretical ideal that management has the authority to determine the method of operations, direct the work force, and make job assignments, whether or not these rights are spelled out in the management rights provision of the agreement.

Unions are sensitive to the need for management to operate its business in the manner that will enable it to compete actively in the marketplace, thus assuring its continuation in business and its ability to provide employment. Sometimes this legitimate management goal requires it to take steps under its management rights authority that are viewed by the union as violations of certain other provisions of the parties' contract. Such disputes are a frequent cause for resort to arbitration.

If the dispute concerns the assignment of new tasks result-ing from operational change, the employer may insist on its right to assign the work to a particular employee or classifi-cation, or the right to create a new classification to perform the disputed work. The union, on the other hand, may argue that the tasks are no different from those being currently per-formed by employees in a particular classification and that the work is rightfully theirs.

The union may even argue that the work is so unique as to require the establishment of a new classification and negotia-tions over the rate to be assigned to employees performing that work. Generally, there is little dispute over the employer's uni-lateral authority to alter the work or introduce new tasks into the work place. It is the impact of that assignment upon exist-ing wages, job jurisdiction, and work load that gives rise to the disputes.

———— **Case** ————

The company employs tool crib attendants in La-bor Grade 1 who prepare drills for metal work. It also employs more highly paid drill press operators in La-bor Grade 6 who use those drills in building metal fix-tures. The pertinent contract provisions read as follows:

Article 2. Management shall have the right to manage its operations and direct the work force, consistent with the terms of this Agreement. . . .

Article 6. When the company establishes a clas-sification the parties shall negotiate its job description and wage rate.

The company purchases an automated drill press that selects and mounts the proper drills and then drills the metal stock with the pressing of a few but-tons. The company seeks to assign the work to the lower paid tool crib attendants and the union files a grievance.

Questions and Comments

(1) *If you were the union, would you prefer to have the new work as a separate classification or in Labor Grade 6? What arguments would you use for each claim?*

On its face, it would seem that assignment of the work to Labor Grade 6 drill press operator could result in the greatest financial benefit to its members, preserving the existing job classifications and protecting against erosion of wage rates.

The argument in support of that position would be the fact that the operator is performing more than drill selection; that the assignment to Labor Grade 1 would eliminate the drill press classification, one over which the parties have traditionally bargained; and that the negotiation of such job description and wage rate over the years constituted recognition of the drill press classification as an integral part of the bargaining unit, thus barring the employer from unilaterally eliminating it in an alleged exercise of its managerial authority.

But the union might also be sensitive to the demands of the company in maintaining its competitive position in the industry, and might be concerned that the new operation might indeed result in the elimination of the Labor Grade 6 position. If it felt threatened that assignment to Labor Grade 1 would result in the layoffs of Labor Grade 6 positions, the union might instead argue for a new labor grade to which both classifications would bid. It might argue that the new operation embodies elements of both Labor Grades 1 and 6; that such combination work is recognized as bargaining-unit work; that it would not be consonant with the company's managerial authority to assign to Labor Grade 1 those elements of Labor Grade 6; and that a new classification should be established with the applicable wage to be negotiated by the parties.

(2) *If you were management, how would you respond?*

Management would probably rely on its inherent right to assign employees and direct the work force. It would assert that the duties of neither Labor Grade 1 nor Labor Grade 6 are immutable; that its assignment of the work to Labor Grade 1 was consistent with the contents of that classification's job description; and that the Labor Grade 6 employees did not own the right to all work involving the type traditionally assigned to Labor Grade 6 employees. Management would further state that the union has not met its burden of showing that the company's action violated any contract provisions.

(3) *If you were the arbitrator, what criteria would you look to in deciding this case?*

The employer's assignment of the new operation to Labor Grade 1 employees constitutes management of its operation as well as an act of direction of its work force. It should follow, therefore, that since both phrases are listed as inherent rights of management, the employer should win. However, it should be recognized that the general language of the management rights clause must give way to more specific language of the other provisions of the contract—i.e., that the proclaimed managerial authority be exercised in a manner consistent with the rest of the agreement.

The other pertinent provision of the agreement, Article 6, reserves to the union the right to negotiate job descriptions and wage rates. But it does not bar the company's right to assign work to those classifications.

Thus, unless the union is able to show that Article 6 or the parties' past practice has resulted in freezing job or machine assignments to a particular classification, the company's right to direct the work force and manage its operations would not conflict with the Article 6 requirement of negotiation, and it would justify the new operation. If the union failed to establish that the new work was beyond the Labor Grade 1 description, the grievance would have to be denied.

If the union showed that some elements of the higher paid classification are now being performed by the Labor Grade 1 employees, the result would be a cutting of the rate and violation of the contractual requirement to maintain negotiated wage rates for certain tasks for the life of the agreement. The arbitrator might propose that the parties renegotiate the wage rate for the new operation or, since some of its elements fall within the Labor Grade 6 classification rather than Labor Grade 1, that the higher rate should be paid until the parties themselves strike a different bargain.

(4) *As arbitrator, how would you rule if the employer elimi-nated Labor Grades 1 and 6 and sought to merge all cov-ered employees into a new Labor Grade 3 classification of automated drill machine operator?*

As in the earlier case, the union bears the burden of prov-ing to the arbitrator that the company's establishment of the new Labor Grade 3 position is violative of the parties' agree-ment. Again, there is little question that the employer has the right to create an additional classification of automated drill operator. Nor is there any real doubt as to the employer's abil-ity to merge the other two existing classifications under its Ar-ticle 2 authority. It would, of course, have to negotiate the rate for that new position.

Most arbitrators endorse the right of the employer to elim-inate classifications where, for example, the work has disap-peared, even if the parties had negotiated such classifications. They would also accept the employer's right to establish a tem-porary new classification and/or wage rate subject to the par-ties' requirements of negotiation thereof. If the parties are un-able to resolve their dispute over the appropriate wage rate for the new classification, then the parties' grievance procedure may embrace the disagreement as a dispute appealable to ar-bitration. At arbitration, the neutral may be authorized to "evaluate" the job (see Chapter 9) and, in certain relation-ships, to set the wage rate.

Employees displaced by the introduction of the new opera-tion would generally have the contractual right to bid into the new classification. Failing such right to bid, such employees might be subject to layoff with a right to bump into positions held by junior employees, usually presuming their ability to handle the work of that classification.

Subcontracting

Subcontracting is the process of "arranging with another firm to make goods or perform services which could be performed by bargaining unit employees with the company's facilities."[2]

There are a number of means by which parties deal with the subcontract issue in the collective bargaining agreement. Arbitrator Donald Crawford identified four general categories of clauses. The first, and that placing the least limitation on management's prerogatives, would be the following:

> If the company determines that bargaining-unit work shall be contracted out, it shall discuss the impact of such decision with the union.

Such a clause requires more than merely "advising" the union, but in no sense requires that there be negotiation or that the union's acquiescence be obtained.

At the other end of the contractual spectrum would be a total prohibition against contracting out:

> There shall be no contracting out of bargaining-unit work absent an emergency, the lack of qualified employees, or mutual agreement by the parties.

Note that any economic consideration on the part of the employer is irrelevant under such language.

Numerous variations exist. Many contracts incorporate a requirement of reasonableness, thereby obligating the employer to utilize bargaining-unit employees for bargaining-unit work whenever possible. Other versions permit subcontracting except when so doing would result in the layoff of bargaining-unit employees.

In any language incorporating judgments based on "reasonableness," disputes will arise as to whether, in fact, the decision in a given case was reasonable. It is also possible that the parties will differ as to what is bargaining-unit work or whether contracting out did, in fact, result in the reduction of a unit employee.

But the real problems in this area stem not from the contract language but from its absence. If nothing is said in the

---

[2]This was the definition suggested by Donald A. Crawford in his superb article, "The Arbitration of Disputes Over Subcontracting," in *Challenges to Arbitration*, Proceedings of the 13th Annual Meeting, National Academy of Arbitrators (Washington, D.C.: BNA Books, 1960), at 51. This article is generally considered indispensable reading for any student of the subject.

labor agreement, does management have the wholly unfettered right to contract out work? The weight of arbitral opinion says "no." That is, even though there is no language in the labor agreement dealing with the subject of subcontracting, arbitrators have concluded that there are certain constraints.

Contrary to the assumption of certain commentators, this results not from a partial abandonment of the reserved rights theory but rather from the conclusion that by recognizing the union and entering into the labor agreement, management has, in fact, bargained away certain rights in the subcontracting area. Sylvester Garrett, then Chairman of the Board of Arbitration of the United States Steel Corporation and United Steelworkers of America, found such limitations inherent in the recognition clause:

> "The inclusion of given individuals in the bargaining unit is determined, not on the basis of *who they are,* but on the basis of the *kind of jobs* which they happen to fill. In view of the fact that the Union has status as exclusive representative of all incumbents of a given group of jobs, it would appear that recognition of the Union plainly obliges the Company to refrain from arbitrarily or unreasonably reducing the scope of the bargaining unit.
>
> "What is arbitrary or unreasonable in this regard is a practical question which cannot be determined in a vacuum. The group of jobs which constitute a bargaining unit is not static and cannot be. Certain expansions, contractions, modifications of the total number of jobs within the defined bargaining unit are normal, expectable and essential to proper conduct of the enterprise. *Recognition of the Union for purposes of bargaining does not imply of itself any deviation from this generally recognized principle.* The question in this case, then, is simply whether the Company's action—either as to window washing or slag shoveling—can be justified on the basis of all relevant evidence *as a normal and reasonable management action in arranging for the conduct of work at the plant.*" (Emphasis added.)[3]

Thus, arbitrators have developed a so-called "implied obligations" theory in the area of subcontracting. The theory is applied in diverse and often remarkable ways. There can be no ready tests as to when a particular subcontracting decision will be violative of these implied obligations. As a general matter, however, arbitrators look to whether the company is somehow undermining the status of the union as collective bargain-

---

[3] *National Tube Co. & U.S.A.,* 17 LA 790, 793 (Garrett 1951).

ing agent by sending the work elsewhere. If the decision is primarily for the purpose of beating union prices or devitalizing the integrity of the bargaining unit, the decision will, more likely than not, be overturned by the arbitrator. Thus, an essential ingredient in most such cases is the concept of good faith. Why did the employer send the work elsewhere? What follows are some criteria that arbitrators examine in attempting to assess the reasonableness of the action in question.

(1) Whether the work is permanent or temporary. A temporary situation poses less of a threat to the continued vitality of the bargaining unit.

(2) The skill and ability of employees to do the work. Are the bargaining-unit employees qualified to do the work in dispute? Have they ever done such work in the shop? Is the work in dispute sufficiently related to their bargaining-unit work to require that it be assumed within existing classifications?

(3) Tools and equipment to do the work. Does the company possess the necessary tools and equipment to carry out the disputed work? Does the company regularly lease, rent, or borrow such tools in its regular operation? Are there sufficient, trained personnel to operate such tools and equipment?

(4) Time and other considerations. Must the work be done by a deadline? Would the assignment of bargaining-unit employees to the task disrupt their ability to fulfill other responsibilities? Would it require unduly long or perhaps contractually prohibited overtime assignments?

(5) Impact on bargaining-unit personnel. Did the subcontracting work result in reductions of overtime or layoffs? Did it delay the permanent recall of laid-off personnel?

Arbitrator Crawford, having examined a sampling of subcontracting awards, summarized the frequent reasons for upholding contracting out:

"The unit employees are busy. The work is temporary. The employer need not hire temporary workers. There has been no layoff or loss of earnings. The employer does not have to postpone the work. Nor change his schedules. Nor does he have to cancel the contract because of a subsequent layoff caused by business conditions. Nor does the company have to recall A to make B available. Nor promote painter helpers to painters jobs. The company is not geared to handling the construction project, and bits of it need not be retained for unit employees to do."[4]

Note that included in the above list is at least one award suggesting that the lack of the company's managerial resources was a proper consideration. Accordingly, it might be held that, while there was sufficient skill and ability among the employees and, moreover, access to the appropriate equipment, the particular project simply overtaxed the company's managerial capabilities.

—— Case ——

A chocolate manufacturing company had utilized a crew of 12 employees to print its wrappers on a flatbed press. It decided to contract out the work when increasing production volume required the utilization of a costly high-speed label-printing operation. It continued to utilize the flatbed printing press and its crew for a portion of the expanded work but the union grieved the fact that the larger printing operation was contracted out.

Questions and Comments

(1) *As the union, what arguments would you raise against the subcontracting?*

Assuming this is a case of good faith subcontracting, the union might argue that the existing equipment is adequate to meet production needs, particularly if extra shifts are called in to run the equipment around the clock; that label printing was originally recognized as core bargaining-unit work; and that to permit its contracting out would deprive bargaining-unit employees of work for which the union is recognized by the company. In preparing its case, the union should determine the cost of the new equipment, the number, cost, and rate of the

---

[4]*Supra* note 2, at 71.

subcontractor's employees, the skills and availability of bargaining-unit employees to do the work, the cost of leasing or buying the new equipment, and the number of laid-off employees who could be recalled or regular employees assigned to overtime if the work was kept in the bargaining unit. It should seek to mount a case showing that it would be to the employer's economic benefit to have the work performed by bargaining-unit employees.

(2) *On behalf of the employer, what arguments would you make defending its action?*

The employer might stress the bona fides of the move; the obstacles (economic, physical, and time) of securing such equipment for the plant; the inability of bargaining-unit employees to handle the new operation; and the fact that assignment to such tasks would detract from the ability of the company to utilize its regular employees in its core function of manufacturing chocolate.

(3) *As arbitrator, what information would you need to make your decision?*

The prime data might include the parties' relationship on prior subcontracting or contract negotiations concerning subcontracting, and the good faith and relations between the parties (including evidence that the union was kept informed of the subcontracting as it evolved). Relative costs and requisite skills for performing the work in the plant would be of interest. The arbitrator might also examine the adequacy of available equipment. Finally, it might be asked whether the subcontracting of the work resulted in any erosion of bargaining-unit personnel, as opposed to, for example, deprivation of overtime opportunities.

(4) *If you are determined that the contracting out had been improper, what remedy would be appropriate?*

If the disputed work could and should have been done by the bargaining unit, the goal of the subcontracting remedy would be to provide deprived employees with such benefits as they would have received had they performed the disputed work. This might entail terminating the subcontracting and computing what the earnings of bargaining unit employees would have been if they had done the work in question. Those employees whose skill and seniority would have made them eligible for the work would be made whole for earnings denied them by means of the employer's actions. The remedy might involve reimbursement of lost overtime wages or payment to laid-off employees who would otherwise have worked. Some arbitrators, however, might forego the issuance of such payments on the grounds that the employer had acted in good faith and should not be penalized. Such a remedy would be tantamount to a cease and desist order with no financial outlay by the employer.

Emergencies and Acts of God

In agreeing to provide certain wages, hours, and working conditions for employees, it is assumed by both parties, although not necessarily guaranteed, that the status quo of work opportunity and employee availability will continue without interruption. Sometimes, however, emergencies arise that prevent the employer from providing work. The plant may lose its power supply or a severe storm or bridge washout may prevent employees from reaching the plant. The storm may, by curtailing most employee availability, also destroy work opportunities for the few who are able to reach the plant.

It is argued by management that one of its managerial prerogatives is to declare exemption from contractual obligations of compensation when an emergency situation or an Act of God occurs. This argument may be based upon specific contract language relieving the employer of its contractual obligations in such circumstances. Even absent such language, arbitrators are generally unwilling to infer a guarantee of work.

Parties do provide guaranteed pay in certain situations. Employees who are called in off-schedule are often promised a certain minimum compensation:

> The employer will provide a minimum of four hours' pay for employees called back after their shift or called in early.

It is also common to provide for situations where work cannot be provided to employees during their normal shift:

> An employee who reports for work, but for whom no work is available, shall be entitled to four hours' pay at his or her regular rate.

Occasionally, even this obligation is qualified to account for emergency situations by providing that the minimum pay will be applicable except where the lack of work is due to an emergency situation. Where parties have specified employer relief in the event of an Act of God or emergency, the arbitrator is frequently called upon to determine if the facts of a given case warrant payment.

 **Case**

At midnight, the main press in the employer's printing plant stops running and, despite the maintenance crew's best efforts, it cannot be fixed. The company announces over the local radio station, hourly until 6 a.m., that there will be no 7 a.m. shift. Nevertheless, several employees report to work and claim a full day's pay or, alternatively, four hours' reporting pay. The labor agreement contains the following provision:

> An employee who reports for work, but for whom no work is available, shall be entitled to four hours' pay at his or her regular rate. This clause shall not be applicable in cases where the employer is prohibited from providing work by an emergency situation.

Questions and Comments

(1) *What should the union's argument be?*

The union would stress the fact that the employees were unaware of the equipment breakdown; that they reported to work in routine fashion; and that the employer is obligated to either find them other work or pay them the requisite day's pay or four hours' reporting pay. This, it would argue, is merely a serious, but nevertheless routine, maintenance problem to be expected in day-to-day operations. It was never the intent of the parties, it would be argued, to have employees act as insurers against this type of eventuality. An emergency must be confined to Acts of God and other unforeseen circumstances of a similar nature.

(2) *What defenses against payment would you make as the employer?*

The employer would argue that the equipment failure was in fact an emergency beyond its control; that it had attempted in good faith to reach the employees to advise them of the no-work situation prior to the start of their shifts; that such efforts fulfilled its obligation; and that since there was no possibility of production that day due to conditions beyond the employer's control, it was relieved of any obligation to pay employees that day.

(3) *As arbitrator, how would you rule?*

This can be a close question. In the final analysis, it can turn on the extent of the mechanical problem and might involve an inquiry into the overall nature of the production setup. Each side has a valid point. If the breakdown was such as should be expected on occasion, it should not reasonably be regarded as an emergency. Thus, despite the employer's good faith efforts to call off the workers, the reporting pay should be required, at least for the initial shift. (After that, one might conclude that employees knew, or should have known, of the shutdown.) But if this breakdown was far beyond the reasonable expectations of the employer, it may be found to have been the type of "emergency" that should release the employer from its obligation under the provision in question.

The above result would probably differ under the following language:

> In the event of an Act of God which interferes with the plant's operation, the employer shall be relieved of any call-in pay obligations.

Overtime Assignment

The traditional reserved rights theory of management rights applied to the issue of overtime assignment means that absent contractual language to the contrary, the employer has the unfettered right to assign employees to overtime work.

A number of collective bargaining agreements have provisions recognizing the right of the employees to reject such overtime assignments. The language may read: "All overtime assignments shall be voluntary," or it may contain some restrictions such as: "Overtime assignments may be refused except in case of emergency." But absent such restrictions, overtime assignments are merely an aspect of management's general rights to schedule work. In practice, the parties will provide for voluntary assignments, at least initially, by means of a rotating overtime list. But failing this, the employer will generally have the right to "force" such assignments. This is usually done in inverse order of seniority, subject to the particular requirements of the job.

Without contract restriction, the employer might be seen as able to assign the overtime work to whichever employee or employees it preferred. Indeed, superior work performance, ready availability, continued stamina over long work hours, and plain old favoritism might well result in overtime assignments being repeated for a few employees to the detriment of others just as willing to work the overtime, but who are not asked.

To overcome potential disparity of treatment, many parties have negotiated contract provisions requiring equitable distribution of available overtime work. A common provision endeavoring to "even out" the distribution of available overtime work reads:

> Overtime shall be distributed on as equitable a basis as possible within the department.

Note that this language refers to "equitable" rather than "equal." Arbitrators have drawn distinctions between the requirement of achieving equality at any given moment as opposed to maintaining a rough equivalence over a period of time.

Arbitrators are frequently called upon to determine if such a contractual standard has been adhered to. In making their determination, they may have to consider

(1) if the disputed work was indeed overtime,
(2) whether "equality" was required and achieved,
(3) whether "as equitably as possible" would excuse special assignments requiring unique skills,
(4) the impact of rejection of a prior overtime call by an employee on that employee's subsequent overtime calls,
(5) how strict compliance will be if one employee is but one or two hours below another in overtime opportunities,
(6) how big a physical area is embraced in the equalization,
(7) the access of employees on different shifts to such overtime,
(8) the number of continuous hours of overtime permitted before one employee is called in to replace another,
(9) the time span within which such equalization is to be attained.

The answers to these many issues are generally imbedded in the parties' overtime practices, but may also be found in the collective bargaining agreement. Overtime distribution rules tend to grow in complexity as problems are confronted by the parties in trying to implement their commitment to the concept of equalization.

—— **Case** ——

Dana Thompson had turned down every request for Friday evening overtime his employer had made in the three years he had been with the company. Late on Friday, November 25, the foreman realized he needed three hours of overtime work and did not ask Thompson, the lowest in overtime hours. Instead, he gave the work to someone with greater overtime hours. Thompson grieved the failure to offer him the overtime. The parties' agreement read as follows:

When overtime work is available it shall be offered first to the employees with the least overtime. Overtime hours shall be equalized by December 31.

Questions and Comments

(1) *What other factual information might be relevant?*

It might be important to know the frequency of the Friday night offerings; whether Thompson had worked all other offered overtime; whether he had been bypassed on prior Fridays without protesting; whether there was an understanding between Thompson and his foreman that excused his being bypassed; whether Thompson's reason for rejecting Friday overtime had changed, and whether that change had been communicated to the foreman; and whether Thompson was indeed available to be offered overtime on the Friday in question.

An arbitrator would also require data on how employees with a history of rejecting overtime had been dealt with in the past; whether the union had knowledge of and waived such bypassings in the past; and whether there had been strict or loose adherence to the notification rules of the parties in the past.

(2) *As arbitrator, how would you rule?*

If the evidence showed there had been strict adherence to the contractual requirement of offering overtime to the employee with the least overtime, and if there was no showing of an expressed waiver by Thompson on being asked for Friday overtime, or that Friday overtime was rare or not offered in a long time, most arbitrators would probably conclude that the employer was obligated to offer the overtime on November 25 even though Thompson had turned down prior Friday overtime offerings. A different result could occur if there was evidence of a prior understanding between Thompson and his foreman that he could not work Friday overtime. If there was such an understanding, then it might have been incumbent upon the grievant to advise his foreman that he would be available for Friday overtime thereafter. If the evidence showed a weekly practice of asking Thompson even though he regularly rejected the offer, most arbitrators would hold that his rejections were for those weeks only and that he had every right to expect to be asked on the Friday in question. However, if the employer could show that the grievant had a consistent prior Friday commitment, such as a religious observance, that always barred his taking the assignment, and that that commitment also precluded his taking the assignment *that* Friday, then most arbitrators would probably find that he could not profit from the employer's omission.

(3) *If the grievant prevails, what remedy would you award?*

The remedy question on overtime equalization has generated considerable controversy. The employer usually argues that a make-up opportunity is all that is required. The union normally claims compensation for the lost overtime hours. The arbitrator's determination will depend upon the likelihood of accomplishing the equalization in an ex post facto fashion. If the violation occurred early in the equalization period and the award was rendered within that same period, then providing another opportunity would be considered as making whole the employee for what he lost, i.e., access to overtime work. This goal is often unattainable, however, if in the period since filing the grievance, the employee has moved to a different equalization unit, or if the composition of the equalization unit has changed so that offering a make-up opportunity adversely impacts on the overtime rights of another employee who might not have been in the original grouping or who might not have "profited" by the earlier error. In this case, the contract calls for equalization by the end of the year. If the award will be rendered in the succeeding year, the equalization "window" is closed. The provision of a "make-up" opportunity would grant Thompson make-up hours that should go to the junior hours employee in the new equalization period, thus violating that employee's entitlement to overtime. In such cases, most arbitrators would find that compensation for the amount of the Friday November 25 overtime work denied to Thompson would be the appropriate remedy.

In constructing overtime lists, seniority is normally used as a criterion for preferred access to available work. The standard is to provide initial access to overtime to the most senior employees, with others being provided subsequent access on a rotation basis to equalize or effect an equitable distribution of available overtime hours, depending upon the contract. The parties usually agree to the size of the group to share in the distribution as well as to the rules for distributing available work. Sometimes they set limits on the number of consecutive hours to be worked, the handling of emergency assignments, the remedy for misassignments, and the time span within which the agreed-upon distribution is to be accomplished.

Maintenance of Standards

Management's reserved rights are constrained, as indicated above, to the extent they are bargained away by the contract terms. They are also limited, on occasion, by terms incorporating unwritten practices. Thus, parties may wish to insure that the past practices or local working conditions that predate the contract are continued, except where expressly modified. In such cases they will negotiate a provision that might read as follows:

Any rights and protections previously enjoyed by employees will continue in effect.

Or

All professional benefits presently enjoyed will continue unless in conflict with the terms of this Agreement.

The most famous local working conditions clause is that known as the "Section 2-B" provision in the steel industry. It reads, in part:

"SECTION 2-B—LOCAL WORKING CONDITIONS

"1. The term 'local working conditions' as used herein means specific practices or customs which reflect detailed application of the subject matter within the scope of wages, hours of work or other conditions of employment and includes local agreements, written or oral, on such matters. Local working conditions now in effect shall remain in effect unless they are in conflict with the rights of employees under this Agreement or are changed by mutual agreement. Employees shall be entitled to process grievances to secure alteration or elimination of any local conditions which deprive them of any benefits under this Agreement."

Note that "local working conditions" are defined in terms of "specific practices or customs." In this manner, the parties agree that a course of conduct repeatedly engaged in over a period of time rises to the level of a binding contract provision.

Arbitrator Saul Wallen identified five "guideposts" applicable to this type of provision.[5] First, an employee has no right to have working conditions established under a contract where they have not previously existed, or where they have been limited. Second, no local working conditions may control any express rights set forth in the agreement. Third, local working conditions that provide benefits "in excess of or in addition to" contractual benefits remain in effect, except as changed by mutual agreement or, significantly, by changed circumstances. The fourth guidepost, referred to in the third, gives the company the right to change or eliminate a local condition if, by exercise of a management right, circumstances underlying the local condition are modified or eliminated. Finally, no local working condition may change or modify any provisions of the labor agreement except by mutual agreement of top management and union officials.

One may note that, in the abstract at least, a written maintenance of standards clause operates much the same as a determination by the arbitrator that a binding past practice exists. Thus, the question arises: Does the existence of this language add anything to otherwise existing rights and obligations? Wallen surmises that in some cases it does; in others, it does not. For example, with respect to areas such as wash-up time, lunch periods, and contracting out, the standards for decision and arbitral results under silent contracts and those with express maintenance of standards provisions appear to have been about the same.[6] By contrast, while most arbitrators would be reluctant to require the continuance of a certain crew size, assuming management concluded the job could be done with less personnel, Wallen found that under the Section 2-B type contract, crew sizes are protected to a considerable degree, assuming no decrease in work load.

---

[5] Wallen, "The Silent Contract vs. Express Provisions: The Arbitration of Local Working Conditions," in *Collective Bargaining and the Arbitrator's Role,* Proceedings of the 15th Annual Meeting, National Academy of Arbitrators (Washington, D.C.: BNA Books, 1962), at 117. These guideposts essentially mirror the series of provisions that follow the introductory portion set forth above.

[6] *Id.* at 130.

Parity Clause

Sometimes parties negotiate a provision that is in effect a "most favored nation" clause. Particularly in multiple-bargaining-unit employment situations, one union (or more) may secure agreement to reopen or modify the negotiated contract during its life if another bargaining unit secures a particular benefit. At times the parity clause will be so general as to reopen the contract whenever a subsequent negotiation with another bargaining unit results in any improvement beyond what the initial contract provided.

Arbitrators called upon to interpret and apply such parity provisions may find themselves interpreting and applying terms of a contract between other parties, and giving meaning to such provisions, thus contributing to what in some cases has been an escalating spiral of benefits secured as the result of such broad language, and incorporating benefits the original parties never contemplated in their initial negotiations. But in so doing, the arbitrator has no mandate other than to give meaning to the provision that the parties themselves agreed to. The economic consequences of such "layering" are the responsibility of the parties who agreed to the provision, not the arbitrator who orders implementation of the parties' language. The provision is relatively rare in modern agreements.

Zipper Clause

Somewhat more prevalent in collective bargaining agreements is a zipper clause. It is, as it suggests, a device for "zipping up" the four sides and corners of the agreement, excluding from coverage any external agreements not made an explicit part of the parties' collective bargaining agreement. In essence, it is the parties' joint recognition that all subjects they wished to discuss have been discussed and that the resulting contract incorporates any and all agreements.

——— Case ———

The company operates 10 plants under one collective bargaining agreement. In 1978, at its Franklin plant, the plant manager and the union signed a local supplementary agreement which, among other things, required the company to bring in a shop steward when an employee was to be disciplined. That agreement continued to be adhered to for the next decade. The parties' national agreement over the years contained a provision entitling the employee to call in a shop steward during discipline, at his option. In the 1982 negotiations, the company secures union agreement to a zipper clause that reads as follows:

> The parties agree that this Contract contains all elements of the parties' understanding. There are no other agreements, except as specifically incorporated herein.

Thereafter, the local in Franklin seeks to set aside a disciplinary penalty because the employer failed to call in a shop steward to the session.

Questions and Comments

(1) *As employer counsel, how would you argue?*

The company representative might argue that the local agreement has only that life given it by the national agreement; that it was the union's burden to revise the national agreement or at least have the national agreement incorporate the Franklin practice; that the failure to do either, with the advent of the zipper clause, overcame any obligation the local management might have had to call the shop steward.

(2) *As union counsel, how would you argue?*

The union would argue that the local provision was one readily negotiated and equally binding on both parties at the Franklin facility; that the parties had long since endorsed that local agreement which merely expanded and was not in any way contradictory to the national agreement; that the zipper clause has its impact solely on the national agreement; and that for the Franklin location, the local standard of shop steward attendance is still controlling.

(3) *How should the arbitrator rule?*

An arbitrator might point out that the grievance and arbitration procedure is part of the national agreement; that his authority was drawn from that national agreement; that the zipper clause in that national agreement restricts the authority to the interpretation and application of that national agreement; that there is nothing in that national agreement endorsing, incorporating by reference, or excluding from the purview of the zipper clause any local agreements or letters of understanding; and that since the local standard for shop steward attendance is not mandated by the national agreement, it is not required in processing cases at that location.

(4) *If the national agreement zipper clause had preceded the local agreement, should the decision be different?*

If the employer had conformed to the agreement, particularly despite intervening national negotiations, one might conclude that the company had, as a matter of past practice, waived its right to invoke the zipper clause—but only insofar as that practice affected proceedings at the Franklin plant.

Arbitrators have made such finding even when the zipper clause had postdated the local agreement, if there was any showing that, after the zipper clause went into effect, the employer at the Franklin location continued to adhere to the prior practice. Here, too, one might find waiver and hold the employer bound to the prior house practice in disciplinary matters.

Savings Clause

The savings clause recognizes that specific terms of the contract may be vulnerable to legal challenge. In the event a particular provision is found to be illegal, the parties may negotiate a provision that will protect the life of the rest of the agreement even if a particular clause is found to be illegal.

—— **Case** ——

The labor agreement for the Feraro Drum Company states in Article 38 as follows:

> The parties agree that any provision in this Labor Agreement found to be illegal shall be severed from the remainder of the Agreement without affecting any remaining obligations.

In 1981, the union grieves the continued implementation by the employer of a departmental seniority plan, set forth in the seniority provisions of the agreement. The employer, for its part, responds that the plan is legal, but even if it is not, the arbitrator has no authority to consider the matter. It points to the arbitration provision of the agreement, which states:

> The arbitrator's function is confined to interpretation and application of the Labor Agreement. She shall have no authority to alter, amend, or modify the terms of the Agreement.

Question and Comment

(1) *Is there a conflict between these two provisions? If so, how is it to be resolved?*

That the parties have attempted to protect the overall stability of the labor agreement by providing for the removal of illegal provisions does not thereby grant the arbitrator authority to make decisions as to legality. The better reading is that, in order for a clause to be excised from the labor contract, it must have been *found* illegal by a court of appropriate jurisdiction. Even then, it is not entirely clear that the arbitrator would have the authority to "enforce" such removal, since she is expressly prohibited from amending the agreement.

5

The Grievance Procedure
and the Arbitration Clause

According to *Basic Patterns in Union Contracts*,[1] grievance proceedings, including arbitration, are included in virtually all contracts sampled. This is predictable. Aside from seniority provisions, agreements covering grievance procedures are widely regarded as among organized labor's most important contributions to the labor-management relationship. Even when there is also access to legal proceedings for enforcement of statutory rights (such as suits involving discrimination matters), the grievance and arbitration process presents the possibility of a satisfactory resolution and, at the least, a determination in arbitration by the parties' own choice of "judge," which is quicker and less expensive than the courtroom route. Because the procedure is of the parties' own molding, except perhaps for some external prerequisites imposed in the public sector, the terms establishing and governing the administration of the grievance and arbitration procedures are vitally important. The focus in this volume is not on the processing of grievances, however. Several sources are available on that topic. Rather, the concern is with the various questions arising when it is necessary to turn to the mutually

---

[1] Washington, D.C.: BNA Books, 1979.

designated third party—the arbitrator—to render final decisions on an issue. Several questions arise in this regard:

(1) substantive arbitrability—What type of dispute have the parties agreed to resolve through arbitration?
(2) procedural arbitrability—Was the grievance properly processed through the preliminary steps, and is it ripe for arbitration?
(3) What powers have the parties given the arbitrator?

Substantive Arbitrability—Defining an "Arbitrable Grievance"

Arbitration can only decide those questions posed by the parties. Absent jurisdiction over the case, an arbitrator will have no authority to inquire into the merits. The U.S. Supreme Court, in the *Steelworkers Trilogy*,[2] expressed the view that arbitrators have authority to decide only those issues which, by agreement of the parties, are ceded to them. When there is a dispute over jurisdiction, an initial inquiry must be made into the scope of the matters that may be properly grieved.

Disputes arise over what is arbitrable. An employee may file a grievance on an issue the parties never contemplated as being within the grievance and arbitration channel. For example, a claim by an employee that a supervisor should be disciplined for some perceived misconduct or a grievance over management choices of a new product line may well be beyond the intended scope of the grievance procedure.

If the parties do not agree to arbitrate a certain class of disputes, the arbitrator has no standing to undertake to do so on his own initiative. If, nonetheless, the arbitrator proceeds to assert jurisdiction over a case over which he has no jurisdiction, and no authority to rule, his overreaching may be appealed to the courts and held invalid. Often, the term "grievance" is defined in a general introductory section of the collective bargaining agreement, rather than in the arbitration clause itself.

---

[2] *United Steelworkers v. Enterprise Wheel & Car Corp.,* 363 U.S. 593 (1960); *United Steelworkers v. Warrior & Gulf Navigation Co.,* 363 U.S. 574 (1960); *United Steelworkers v. American Mfg. Co.,* 363 U.S. 564 (1960).

But wherever the definition is set forth, it must be carefully examined to interpret and apply properly the arbitration clause.

Some parties choose to distinguish between those issues that may be grieved and pursued only through the lower steps of the grievance procedure as opposed to other issues that may be brought all the way to binding arbitration.

A grievance may be defined in the most narrow terms, covering appeals from only some of the employer's actions:

> Grievances shall be limited to disciplinary matters involving warning, suspension, or discharge of an employee.

This language reflects the parties' agreement that *only* disputes concerning discipline may be arbitrated. Questions may arise as to whether management's actions in terminating an employee are disciplinary. Under the language cited above, an employee terminated for failure to return to work promptly after recall from layoff might not have access to the grievance procedure if it were demonstrated that the termination arose as a matter of contract operation rather than in response to a disciplinary event. (See Chapter 7, which covers contractual terminations.)

—— **Case** ——

The Amalgamated Widget Company has a collective bargaining agreement that states in part:

> Grievances shall be limited to questions concerning the discipline or discharge of an employee.

On May 15, John Jones submits his resignation to his supervisor. That evening, having second thoughts about resigning, Jones calls his supervisor and asks him not to transmit the letter. The supervisor responds that the letter has already gone to the appropriate officials, but that Jones should check back in the morning. The next morning, Jones finds that the company has acted with remarkable efficiency and speed—a letter is already awaiting him accepting his resignation. He grieves. The company contends that the matter is not arbitrable.

Questions and Comments

(1) *What are the respective arguments of the parties?*

The company would argue that the language in question is clearly limited to situations involving employee misconduct and a challenge to the disciplinary response, including discharge. The very term "discharge" itself, says the employer, connotes a disciplinary situation as opposed to, for example, "resignation" or even "termination" of an employee.

The union responds that, had the parties understood the term "discharge" to imply a disciplinary situation, it would have been unnecessary to draft the language in terms of "discipline or discharge." Rather than infer a redundancy, says the union, it is incumbent upon the arbitrator to assume the parties mean to provide some greater access to the grievance procedure than suggested by the company.

(2) *How should the arbitrator respond?*

In the common parlance of labor relations, the term "discharge" is normally understood to be a disciplinary response initiated by the employer to remove the employee from the payroll. The term "termination" is generally employed in a more generic sense and is applicable to, for example, resignations, voluntary quits, and other separations from the employment rolls that occur for reasons other than discharge. But the possibility for confusion ought to be recognized, for "termination" may be viewed simply as a more polite reference to discharge. Moreover, in the language set forth above, if "discharge" is, in fact, to be limited to instances of discipline, the language is arguably redundant, as the union suggests.

Thus, the parties are well advised to be careful in considering the intended scope of the grievance procedure and explicitly manifesting their mutual intent. Language such as that set forth earlier, which limits grievances to "disciplinary matters involving warning, suspension, or discharge" is clearly reflective of the intent to incorporate a more restrictive grievance procedure.

Grievance procedures may also be exceptionally broad, encompassing complaints that arise even beyond the contract. Public sector labor agreements often encompass disputes over any claimed violation of law, regulation, or policy—thereby incorporating by reference not only the agreed-upon terms of the labor contract but also all applicable legislation.

The employer is more likely to raise a challenge to arbitrability, inasmuch as the union is normally the grieving party. But, in certain cases, the union may demand that a particular subject be held nonarbitrable. Arbitration is often seen as the quid pro quo for a no-strike agreement, and the union may wish to retain its strike rights even at the expense of giving up the right to arbitrate certain disputes. As one commentator has noted, a finding of nonarbitrability may mean that the dispute becomes one over which the union may conduct an authorized strike under a clause permitting strikes over matters not subject to the grievance procedure.[3] This is underscored by the rule announced by the Supreme Court in *Boys Markets Inc. v. Retail Clerks Union, Local 770.*[4]

At times, there may be more than one provision in an agreement relating to arbitrability. For example, the parties may have negotiated a rather broad definition clause that on its face seems to contemplate a virtually unlimited scope of arbitrability. However, restrictions may be imposed elsewhere in the contract. Thus, a clause in the wage article of the agreement may effectively bar grievances on that subject:

> Management determination of wage rates for new positions shall not be challenged through the grievance procedure.

Although it might be argued that the ban against wage grievances is incompatible with the broader scope of the arbitration provision, most arbitrators would hold that the specific language of the wage article overcomes the more general language of the grievance definition, and that the wage complaint would be excluded from the grievance and arbitration procedures.

Another restriction may arise by virtue of the parties having agreed that only certain cases will progress through the en-

---

[3] Fairweather, *Practice and Procedure in Labor Arbitration* (Washington, D.C.: BNA Books, 1973).
[4] 398 U.S. 235 (1970).

tire grievance procedure. While parties may see the grievance and arbitration process as therapeutic in nature, they desire not to risk the possibility that every complaint, no matter how petty, might find its way to arbitration. At the same time, they recognize the virtue of discussing and possibly even resolving matters which, while minor, may nevertheless constitute a source of continuing irritation within the work force. This is accomplished by fashioning contract language providing that, while all matters may be processed through the lower steps of the grievance procedure, only certain disputes may be appealed all the way to final and binding arbitration. Accordingly, the parties will agree to language that contains a broad grievance definition but continues on to state, for example:

> Grievances challenging the employer's wage rates or new positions shall not be appealed to arbitration.

Note that, compared to the language set forth above, this provision admits a wage complaint to the grievance procedure, but specifies that it shall not be appealed to final and binding arbitration. This means that, failing resolution through discussion at the lower steps of the grievance procedure, the employer's determination will stand. Recall, however, that it may also mean that the union may have retained the right to strike over such grievances, assuming the strike right had otherwise been bargained away in return for final and binding arbitration.

Another example of a limitation on arbitral authority may arise in the area of remedies. Consider the following provisions:

> The parties agree that participation in a strike during the term of this Agreement will be grounds for discharge. In an arbitration on such question, the sole issue for the arbitrator will be whether an employee had, in fact, participated in the strike.

In this agreement, the parties made participation in the strike grounds for discharge and excluded from the arbitrator's authority the right to decide appropriateness of the penalty imposed by the employer on such participants. In this case, the arbitrator's authority is limited to the fact question of whether an employee had been guilty of the prohibited conduct. Once having made that decision, he or she would be powerless to consider the appropriateness of the penalty, and the employer's discipline would stand, assuming the employer found the employee had, indeed, participated. Such was the intent of the parties. It is not within the arbitrator's province to decide issues that the parties specifically exclude from his or her purview.

Probationary Employees

Parties often limit access to arbitration not only by restricting the arbitrator's authority but also by confining eligibility to grieve or appeal to arbitration to nonprobationary employees. It is usually assumed that the employer has the right to terminate a new employee during his or her probationary period. Although this traditional right is readily accepted in private sector employment with a 30- or 60-day probationary period, it tends to be subject to greater challenge as the break-in period extends. In the public sector, where longer probationary periods are common, employers have occasionally sought union agreement to language specifically excluding probationers from the grievance procedure. Other contracts grant access to early steps but foreclose appeals to arbitration. Still others limit the probationer to contract interpretation questions only. Job tenure still remains within the sole discretion of the employer.

In public education, where renewal of employment contracts of nontenured teachers is frequently a matter of statutory delegation of authority to school boards, nontenured teachers may have the same rights as their tenured colleagues to grieve and arbitrate questions of contract violations. But they are usually restricted to the right to challenge only procedural aspects of nonrenewal, with decisions on the renewal itself reserved to the employer. Similarly, in the case of tenured teachers, where removal is usually governed by statute or rules established by a state board of education, grievability and arbitrability are likely to be restricted to procedural matters such as form or timing of notices, times for appeal, etc. Many public sector agreements stipulate that matters for which expressed statutory appeals exist shall not be arbitrated.

——— **Case** ———

Sarah Beth Lukin had been with the company for three weeks when she noticed she had been denied $4.80 of overtime pay. She grieved under the parties' agreement, which defined the probationary period as 45 days but contained no specific reference to grievability during that period.

Assume that the collective bargaining agreement contains the following language:

> The employer shall have the right to discipline and discharge probationary employees. Such actions shall not be pursued through the grievance procedure.

The employer moved to have the grievance dismissed on the grounds giving rise to the instant arbitration.

Questions and Comments

(1) *If you were the company, what would you argue?*

The employer would contend that the contract was intended to apply to permanent employees; that a probationer had no rights under the agreement until the forty-sixth day of employment, when she became a regular employee; and that the probationary period entitled the employer to terminate the grievant for any cause. Since the employer could have avoided the case by simply terminating the grievant, it should not be held to task for a mere allegation of overtime underpayment.

(2) *What would the union argue?*

The union would contend that the contract does not bar access to the grievance procedure for probationary employees or restrict access to those with 45 or more days' seniority. While the grievant may be vulnerable in terms of discipline or discharge, she is entitled, and the union may proceed on her behalf, to enforce the contract.

(3) *If you were the arbitrator, how would you rule?*

Although some arbitrators might hold that being in probationary status deprives a new employee of any right to challenge an employer's actions through the grievance procedure—whether disciplinary or contractual—most arbitrators would hold that such total prohibition of access to the grievance procedure must be spelled out to be enforced. Absent such a blanket prohibition, most arbitrators would find that being the probationer does not deprive an employee of the right to challenge an improper wage payment. To rule otherwise would be tantamount to authorizing exclusion of the individual from all negotiated benefits.

—— **Case** ——

Consider the following language:

> During the first 60 days of employment, an employee shall be on probation. His or her continued job tenure during such time shall be at the sole discretion of the company.

During his first month on the job, Michael Sewell returns late from lunch by two minutes and is given a two-day suspension. He grieves. The union makes the following arguments. First, it notes that no one in the plant's 100-year history has ever been suspended for a late return from lunch on the first offense. Individuals who repeatedly show up late are first warned verbally, then in writing, then suspended. As to access to the grievance procedure, the union notes that the purpose of the probationary period is for management to be able to render an objective evaluation as to the individual's work capabilities. Denying access to the grievance procedure, says the union, is simply reflective of the parties' intent that the individual may be terminated simply on the employer's judgment that this person cannot fulfill the basic employer requisites. But that discretion may not be interpreted as granting the employer unfettered rights to impose any type of discipline, without regard to the demands of fair treatment. In essence, then, the union distinguishes necessary judgments as to work capabilities from disciplinary situations.

The employer responds that, so long as it could impose the ultimate termination penalty, it is similarly free to discipline without fear of challenge in the grievance procedure. Even if the union's claims are correct as to disparate and unfair treatment, says the employer, the matter may not be arbitrated. Indeed, if the union's claims are correct, the employer would be restricted even as to discharge situations. Assumably, the union might argue that, while the employer could terminate for general lack of ability, a disciplinary discharge would have to be for cause. That was clearly beyond what was intended in negotiating significantly limited rights for probationary employees.

Question and Comment

(1) *If you were the arbitrator, how would you rule?*

There is something to be said for both sides' positions in this case. However, the majority of arbitrators will conclude that, while a probationary employee may have access to the grievance procedure over contractual questions (unless the parties have specifically agreed to the contrary), the right to terminate without cause will include the right to take lesser disciplinary action without being held to the just cause standard during the probationary period.

There are those parties who simply opt for a wide-open grievance procedure that accommodates all types of disputes. Such contracts may define a grievance as follows:

> A grievance is any dispute, complaint, or problem faced by an employee at work.

Another version is as follows:

> A grievance is any dispute that may arise as to an employee's wages, hours, and/or working conditions, whether or not covered by this Agreement.

The Foreign Service Act of 1980, which controls, among other things, the grievance procedure for Foreign Service officers, provides an example of a grievance procedure with virtually unlimited breadth:

> "Except as provided in subsection (b), for purposes of this chapter, the term 'grievance' means any act, omission, or condition subject to the control of the Secretary which is alleged to deprive a member of the Service who is a citizen of the United States of a right or benefit authorized by law or regulation or which is otherwise a source of concern or dissatisfaction to the member, including—...."[5]

Although such provisions may stimulate an overabundance of grievances, there are those who believe that freedom in airing gripes by such a procedure is helpful to clear the air, find trouble spots in the enterprise, and assure the employee that he or she has had a full "single day in court." Such parties view the procedure as therapeutic by channeling dissatisfaction into the parties' internal resolution system.

As was discussed in Chapter 3, these broadly drawn systems are not without their perils. By inviting an arbitrator to consider external matters, including laws, the parties are requiring legal, as opposed to purely contractual, interpretation by the neutral. These may be skills that are beyond the particular expertise of the arbitrator. And, the parties themselves may be unprepared to argue the vast body of statutory and common law precedent that may surround the legal questions. Moreover, one may reasonably question whether private arbitrators should become involved in interpreting and applying public law.

Fears that an arbitrator may rule on matters that are recognized by management and labor as properly within the unilateral control of the employer or governed by external law can be overcome by limiting the appealability of such complaints to arbitration by language such as:

> Only those grievances that involve the interpretation and/or application of this Agreement may be appealed to the arbitration step.

This is the most common approach to overall jurisdiction. It has the benefit of admitting the large bodies of contractual or

---

[5] Foreign Service Act of 1980, 22 U.S.C. §4131, Sec. 1101(2)(1).

disciplinary disputes that may rise under a contract while at the same time not holding open too broad a door for disputes that may be well beyond the confines of the industrial context.

Procedural Arbitrability—Processing the Grievance

In addition to specifying those matters properly subject to arbitration, most collective bargaining agreements also recognize the need for inspiring and assuring expeditious handling of grievances by incorporating time limits and procedures relevant to filing of complaints and subsequent processing through the lower steps up to arbitration.

Negotiated requirements of form and timing grievances and appeals are equally as important as the substantive rights set forth in the contract. The arbitrator is bound by all the provisions of the contract—not merely those he or she believes to be important. The arbitrator cannot pick and choose which provisions to enforce, for to do so would constitute a rewriting of the agreement which is beyond the neutral's authority.

While an arbitrator might prefer to decide a case on its merits, one is duty bound to adhere to the procedural as well as the substantive provisions of a contract. Most arbitrators, however, believe that procedures should be applied no more strictly by them than they are by the parties. Thus, when parties are lax in their own enforcement of procedures, the arbitrator may well find a waiver of the right to challenge the procedural arbitrability; the arbitrator will then proceed to rule on the substantive issue raised by the grievance.

Form of the Grievance

Collective bargaining agreements may require, for example, that a grievance be in writing, that it be signed by both the grievant and the shop steward, and that it cite the particular contract provision in dispute. If the parties have been consistent in demanding and fulfilling such requirements—if proper format has been uniformly and meticulously adhered to—arbitrators will follow suit. But if the evidence shows the employer has accepted and processed grievances lacking the two signatures, or failing to cite the pertinent provision, the arbitrator may find a waiver of the negotiated restrictions, thus permitting consideration of the merits of the case. In certain cases, a grievant will "substantially," but not "fully," comply with requirements of form. Thus, for example, a grievant may cite the wrong paragraph of the relevant article in the grievance. An arbitrator may be hard-pressed to void a grievance on that basis. If, notwithstanding an erroneous listing of the disputed section, the matter has been fully aired at the lower steps of the grievance procedure, arbitrators have often found that the case is properly arbitrable. Arbitrators would hold that by having fully discussed the correct provision during the grievance process, any disadvantage the employer may have claimed from the miscitation has been obviated.

Similarly, if there has been variation from contractual time limits, with the employer accepting grievances or appeals after the deadline or, indeed, in responding to grievances after the time limits set forth for such replies, arbitrators have also held that there has been a "liberal" application of the time limits and thereby considered timely a grievance which, on strict application of the agreement, would otherwise be excluded for tardiness. It is in these cases that the doctrine of "substantial compliance" is most often invoked.

It is not unusual to have a provision stating that failure of the union to appeal will result in forfeiture of the grievance, while a like failure on the part of the employer will merely result in the case being advanced automatically to the next step of the procedure. This result may even obtain in the absence of express language, since management's failure to answer within time limits may be interpreted as a denial, in which case the grievance still moves forward as if a denial had, in fact, been issued. Thus, the language will provide, for example:

> Upon receipt of management's answer at the first step, if the union is dissatisfied, it must file the grievance at the second step within 10 days or forfeit its right to proceed.

In some cases, however, the parties have sought to force a response by management by incorporating a waiver clause that cuts both ways:

> Noncompliance with the time limits (or mutual extension thereof) on the part of either party shall result in forfeiture of that party's position.

Such a provision is not without its drawbacks. Management may avoid a forfeiture simply by issuing a blanket denial. Similarly, the union may resort to "form pleadings" wherein matters are advanced from step to step without any substantial exchange of views or information. On the other hand, to the extent such a clause may inspire attention to a matter which would otherwise have gone unnoticed, it may be of value.

Time limits in grievance procedures, then, are important and should be so regarded by the parties, as they are by the arbitrators. Most agreements provide relatively short periods within which grievances must be filed and subsequently processed through the grievance procedure. Such time limits are in conformity with the implicit goal of prompt investigation and rapid resolution of the parties' disputes.

Despite best efforts, parties will often incorporate substantial ambiguities that arbitrators must resolve in applying the procedural rules.

——— Case ———

The grievance procedure requires:

Appeals to the third step must be made within five (5) days of the second-step answer.

The evidence establishes the following: (1) the second-step meeting was held January 10; (2) the supervisor told the union the appeal was denied at that level; (3) a letter to that effect was mailed January 11 and received by the union January 13; (4) the union mailed its appeal to the third step January 18; and (5) it was received by the personnel director January 20. The appeal was refused as being tardy and the union challenged the rejection.

Questions and Comments

(1) *If you were the union, what evidence would you seek to support your position? How would you argue?*

The union spokesperson would be well advised to prepare testimony and supporting documentation that would establish (1) that the letters were received and sent on the dates it alleges; (2) that the Postal Service has been the accepted vehicle for such exchanges; and (3) that written, rather than oral, responses were the established practice. In addition, it should examine records of prior grievances to show that the company had accepted without protest grievances which were sent on the fifth day following union receipt of the written second-step answer. Above all, the union's case would be strengthened by evidence that the company had accepted responses more than five days old or that the company had been tardy in its own responses to the time limits set forth in the agreement.

If the evidence showed the employer had been tardy itself or had accepted tardy responses, the union would presumably argue that the company had acquiesced in any format of relatively loose time limits—or indeed, waived the deadlines entirely.

Even if the evidence could not support such an argument of waiver, the union could argue the time limits were, indeed, met in this case and the written, rather than the oral, denial was the triggering event, for otherwise there would have been no need for the January 11 company letter. Accordingly, the five days for response ran from the receipt of the company denial and, consistent with prior mail practice, the response was timely. It would presumably also be argued that the provision refers to appeals being "made" rather than "received by the company" within the five days.

(2) *How would management respond?*

Management would likewise seek to offer testimony or evidence of past practice showing strict adherence to the time limits and demonstrating that the time for appeal tolled from the oral denial rather than from the letter of January 11. It would also attempt to show that such appeals had been routinely "received" by the company by the fifth day. In any event, it might be argued that the parties agreed to strict, explicit time limits for appeals, that attainment of that goal is better achieved by running the time limits from the oral denial, and that the time gap in this case was 10 days. Evidence that the company had, in the past, denied grievances under similar circumstances, without protest by the union, might be submitted.

(3) *How should the arbitrator rule?*

As indicated earlier, an arbitrator would accept evidence showing laxity on the part of the parties in adhering to strict time limits. However, if the evidence showed a clear practice of the five days running from the oral denial or running until the actual delivery of the appeal, the arbitrator should properly be obligated under contract language to conclude that the appeal was untimely. The preferable result would be, taking the facts as presented without added input, to conclude that the formal response from the company was the triggering item and that the union was entitled to the same vehicle of mail delivery for its response. Since the contract stipulated five days for consideration of whether or not to appeal, the union was entitled to use its full time before responding.

(4) *Would the decision be different if the company had received the appeal at the third step, responded that the grievance lacked merit, and not raised a timeliness challenge until the arbitration hearing?*

If the company believed the grievance was untimely and therefore barred from consideration on the merits, arbitrators have held that it was incumbent upon the company to so state in its third-step answer. In such cases, the arbitrators have reasoned that the failure to do so unfairly leads the union to conclude that the grievance has been accepted as timely, eliminating the need for any further investigation or preparation of the case with respect to procedures. Other arbitrators have concluded that timeliness is an essential ingredient in jurisdiction and that failure to raise it at the lower steps of the grievance procedure does not amount to a waiver.

In any event, the company would have been wise to state its continuing objection to timeliness, reserving its rights on that issue while proceeding to a discussion of the case on the merits, in the hope that resolution of the substantive issue would settle the matter.

Many contracts provide that grievances must be filed within a certain number of days after the contested incident out of which the grievance arises. Such provisions place on the grievant and union the requirement of policing contract violations. Thus, failure to provide extra payment for overtime work may be a violation that occurred when the overtime work was performed, and an employee would have until, say, five days thereafter to grieve the denial of extra compensation. But if the grievant were not paid until the tenth day after performance of overtime work, most arbitrators would hold that the "incident" giving rise to the grievance was not the work date but, rather, the discovery (at the time of receiving the paycheck) that the appropriate payment had not been made.

This result might obtain even if the employer had stated on the work day that the employee would not be paid for the extra work. One might argue that the employer's "notification" should be considered as the grievable incident, giving the grievant only the initial five days to appeal. On the other hand, the employee might well be found to have acted reasonably in giving the employer a chance to change its mind before filing a formal grievance.

Parties frequently relax contractual time limits by language setting the time limit for grieving, not woodenly within "X" days after the incident but rather

Within "X" days after the incident or the employee's first knowledge thereof.

Or

Within "X" days after the incident or after the aggrieved became aware or should have become aware of the alleged violation.

The distinction here is between *actual* as opposed to *constructive* knowledge. In the first example, the grievant who did not examine the paycheck for the discrepancy on the fifth day but did notice it three weeks later might well be found to have filed in a timely fashion. In the second example, however, after having worked the overtime in that pay period, the arbitrator might rule that the grievant had an obligation to determine whether or not payment had been made in the covering paycheck—that she "should have been aware" of the deficit since she had received "constructive" knowledge of the deficit.

A related question occurs in cases of alleged "continuing violations." (One veteran labor practitioner has suggested—tongue firmly embedded in cheek—that a continuing violation is any one where the grievance is late.) For example, if an employee is upgraded to a higher rated job but continues to receive the lower compensation, a grievance would normally be expected after the initial paycheck disclosed the shortage. The argument is made that even if the grievance is not filed until a month later, it is still alive because the violation continues. On the one hand, if the contract breach continues, it is appropriate to accept the grievance, although a minority of arbitrators may hold the grievant to a higher standard of policing the violation.

But even assuming adoption of a continuing violation approach, the grievant may be found to have forfeited back pay by waiting past "first knowledge." Disputes over the extent of financial obligations in these situations have led many parties to incorporate specific limitations on retroactivity. Thus, referring once more to the first example of contract language above, the provision might be expanded as follows:

> Within "X" days after the incident or the employee's knowledge thereof, provided, however, that retroactive monies, if any, shall not extend beyond 30 days.

The existence of a limitation on retroactivity serves as a stimulus to prompt filing.

Procedure at the Hearing

Often management will raise a challenge to arbitrability as a preliminary matter. In most cases, the parties will proceed to argue the arbitrability aspect of the dispute, then proceed to hear the merits. The arbitrator's obligation under those circumstances is to respond first to the arbitrability question. If the employer prevails, there must be no answer on the merits, for the arbitrator has concluded that he or she is without any jurisdiction. Only if the conclusion is that the matter is arbitrable may the neutral proceed with the merits.

Two practical issues warrant further discussion in this regard. First, there are limited instances when arbitrators (and courts as well) have, in effect, "ducked" the jurisdiction question and answered the merits. For obvious reasons, this only occurs when the grievance itself is without merit. From a technical standpoint, this is questionable practice, since if the matter is not arbitrable, the arbitrator is without authority to give any answer. Realistically, however, cases arise where the jurisdiction question is long and complex, and where its resolution would require substantial time on the part of the arbitrator and consequent expense to the parties. Yet, the case itself may be frivolous. In such instance, it makes little sense for the arbitrator to indulge in a talmudic recitation of sophisticated contract analysis only to conclude the grievant was, indeed, properly fired for say, kidnapping the company president. It is for this reason arbitrators have, on occasion, ignored the jurisdiction question with language such as "even assuming, without deciding, that the matter is arbitrable, the conclusion is that the grievance must be denied." It should be readily apparent that, while practical in certain instances, it is hardly to be recommended as an accepted technique.

On more than rare occasions, an employer will request a decision on arbitrability prior to proceeding with the case on the merits. This is invariably a delicate situation. There is no inherently apparent answer to this dilemma. On the one hand, the union wishes to have the case heard in its entirety. On the other hand, jurisdiction of the matter is a serious question; if the arbitrator has no authority to render a decision, substantial time and effort may be saved by receiving that answer first. Additionally, an employer should not be required to appear in a forum that lacks jurisdiction to decide the matter.

Certain commentators suggest that the employer's request for an adjournment should be approved if the employer has previously notified the union that such request will be made. This "rule" is rational—it is not necessarily controlling.

Arbitrators have considered many factors under such circumstances, including the length of the hearing, the expenses involved in travel and obtaining witnesses, and the nature of the issues. Considering that the employer will, after all, receive a decision on jurisdiction before proceeding to the merits, arbitrators have concluded that the entire matter, both procedural and substantive, will be aired.

Powers of the Arbitrator

Most labor agreements include standard language affirming the well-accepted notion that arbitrators are proscribed from "altering, amending, or otherwise changing the terms of the parties' agreement." Their job is to interpret and apply the terms of the parties' agreement, not to rewrite it. This is a basic and rational requirement. It is the parties' job to formulate the terms of their bargain. The arbitrator functions solely to resolve disputes as to such interpretation, or to apply the agreement when the employer is called to task for failing to do so. As noted by Dean Harry Shulman, the arbitrator "is not a public tribunal imposed upon the parties by superior authority which the parties are obliged to accept. He has no general charter to administer justice [for a community] which transcends the parties. He is rather part of a system of self-government created by and confined to the parties."[6]

It might be argued that a certain amount of "amending" occurs each time an arbitrator voices his or her opinion on the proper construction of disputed language. Yet, there is a distinct difference between interpreting an agreement and amending it. The arbitrator's role is to apply the various provisions of a contract to a given set of facts that arise subsequent to the conclusion of the parties' negotiations—to fill in the narrow cracks left open in the contract language. In doing so, the goal must be to achieve that result most consistent with the standards the parties themselves establish. The critical factor is that the arbitrator must set forth what the agreement says according to the arbitrator's reading of the parties' intent, and not what the agreement *should* say in the arbitrator's personal view of industrial relations.

Arbitrators are often restricted to a particular set of issues in the industrial relationship, such as discharge disputes (and, in some cases, discharge only—not lesser discipline) or other selected areas. Arbitrators may also be restricted as to the remedy they may apply in cases of breach. The accepted notion (both in general contract law and in labor contract interpretation) is that the grievant who prevails in a case is to be put

---

[6]Shulman, "Reason, Contract and Law in Labor Relations," 69 *Harv. L. Rev.* 999, 1016 (1955).

in the same position he or she would have been in had the employer adhered to the requirements of the contract. In discipline and discharge cases, parties normally give the arbitrator broad discretion to fashion appropriate remedies.

A company and a union in the automobile industry, for example, take particular pains to specify the powers of the umpire, which vary according to the nature of the case. In subcontracting cases, the parties provide that

> "the umpire can only provide a remedy where he finds that (1) a violation of the express commitment [concerning subcontracting] has been established, (2) the established violation resulted from the exercise of improper judgment by management, and (3) ... [an] employee who customarily performs the work in question has been laid off or was allowed to remain on layoff as a direct and immediate result of work being subcontracted. The umpire's remedy shall be limited to back wages for the parties at interest as defined in [another portion] of this paragraph."[7]

The approach to discipline cases differs:

> "The corporation delegates to the umpire full discretion in cases of discipline for violation of shop rules, or discipline for violation of Strikes, Stoppages, and Lock-Out Section of the Agreement."[8]

Prior to their 1977 agreement, a steel company and the union had provided that, in discipline cases, the umpire was confined to an "all or nothing" decision. Either the penalty was to be sustained in its entirety or overturned. But in that agreement, the parties changed their standard to provide, among other things, that even when there *was* just cause for, say, discharge, the umpire could modify the penalty in response to observed circumstances. Indeed, the parties gave the arbitration board full discretion to modify the extent of the penalty even where the board found the action had been for proper cause:

> "Should it be determined by the board (of arbitrators) that an employee has been suspended or discharged for proper cause, the board shall have jurisdiction to modify the degree of discipline imposed by the company. In the event the board modifies the discipline, the board shall have discretion to reduce or not require the company to pay the compensation provided in

---

[7] 1976 Labor Agreement between General Motors and the United Auto Workers, Paragraph 46.
[8] *Id.* at Paragraph 47.

the immediately preceding paragraph if, in its judgment, the facts warrant such an award."[9]

Questions of remedy often become the most difficult part of a discipline contract interpretation case. Some parties opt to remove all discretion from the neutral in such cases. An agreement in the utility industry sets forth the "power or jurisdiction of arbitrators" as follows:

"No arbitrator shall have power or jurisdiction to modify the Company's action. The arbitrator shall either find that the Company's action was not without just cause, in which event the suspension, demotion or discharge shall be sustained in full; or that the suspension, demotion or discharge was without just cause, in which event the treatment of the case shall be as set forth in Section 10.03 of this Article."[10]

Section 10.03, referred to above, specifies in substantial detail the terms of the reinstatement and reimbursement:

"1. In a discharge case, the employee shall receive his basic weekly wage rate for the time lost (including pay lost during the ten (10) day suspension period) less the amount of any termination pay received from the Company, and unemployment compensation received or receivable, and any amount paid to or receivable by the employee as wages in other employment. If the employee received a termination payment and the number of weeks since the date of discharge is less than the number of weeks upon which the payment was based, less vacation, if any, the amount paid to the employee for the excess number of weeks shall be considered as an advance to him by the Company. Repayment shall be made by the employee on a weekly basis satisfactory to the Company until the amount is fully paid, but the employee shall not be required to repay each week at a rate in excess of 10% of his basic weekly wage rate.
"The employee shall also receive:

"a) reimbursement for premiums paid by him from the date of discharge for insurance coverage that does not exceed coverage provided under the Company's Basic Medical Expense Plan, Extraordinary Medical Expense Plan and Group Life and Accidental Death or Dismemberment Insurance Program;
"b) insurance coverage retroactive to the date of discharge for uninsured medical expenses actually in-

---

[9] 1977 Agreement between Jones & Laughlin Steel Corporation and the United Steelworkers of America, Paragraph 8.4.
[10] 1980 Labor Agreement between the New York Telephone Company and the Communications Workers of America, Paragraph 10.03.

curred that would have been covered under the Company's Basic Medical Expense Plan and Extraordinary Medical Expense Plan; and

"c) reimbursement for the amount of discounted telephone service lost during the period of discharge.

"2. In a suspension case, the employee shall receive his basic weekly wage rate for the time lost less the amount of any unemployment compensation received or receivable, and any amount paid to or receivable by the employee as wages in other employment.

"3. In a demotion case, the employee shall be made whole for the difference in basic weekly wage rates for the period of demotion, including any applicable differentials."[11]

The above-quoted provision is unusually comprehensive in its scope. In general, it follows the accepted notion of putting the employee in the position he or she would have had had the improper discharge, suspension, or demotion not occurred.

Parties sometimes impose other limitations on the arbitrator's remedy authority. As noted in Chapter 4, in cases involving improper distribution of overtime, for example, the labor agreement may require a monetary compensation rather than a makeup opportunity or, to the contrary, may specifically exclude compensation, requiring that the remedy be limited to priority access to subsequent overtime. Naturally, where neither restriction is negotiated, the arbitrator granted authority to formulate a remedy by the parties' submission to arbitration has the freedom to embrace either approach consistent with the parties' prior practice or, absent that, his or her concept of an equitable adjustment.

The formula of placing the grievant in the position he should have occupied, or "making whole," is a "compensatory" approach which, by definition, precludes imposition of punitive damages unless the parties have negotiated them. On occasion, they do, such as in a contract which states:

In the event the employer fails to call in an employee for available overtime to which he is entitled, he shall be granted a full eight hours' pay.

In this case, the eight hours' pay has no necessary correlation to the amount of hours lost and may, in a given case, amount to

---

[11]*Id.*

little more than a "fine" on the employer for failing to abide by the contract's requirements. As a general matter, punitive damage provisions are relatively rare and arbitrators, of course, are barred from legislating them.

It is also unusual to find "consequential" damage agreements. A wrongfully discharged employee may suffer numerous financial problems, for example, as a consequence of being deprived of income between discharge and reinstatement. Car or house payments may lapse, foreclosures may occur; the possible chain of nightmares is obvious. Yet, it is virtually unheard of for the parties or arbitrators to account for these consequential damages.

In part, this explains the reluctance of many arbitrators to grant interest on back pay awards. While it is true that a grievant may have lost the "use" of the money for the interim period, this is often viewed as another consequential damage which the parties had not contemplated as accompanying a lost wage award. Some arbitrators, on the other hand, will note (and follow) the practice of the NLRB, which is to grant such interest. As noted earlier, federal sector legislation also contemplates that arbitrators may award attorneys' fees.[12]

Parties also employ the arbitration section to regulate other aspects of the grievance procedure. In most cases, arbitration clauses provide that parties will split all fees and reasonable expenses. But in some instances, the contract will reflect a "loser pay all" provision.

> All costs and fees of the arbitrator and court reporter, if any, shall be borne by the losing party.

Parties should incorporate such a clause only after extensive deliberation. It may have the virtue of saving the "innocent" party the expense of arbitration. On the other hand, such language often results in discouraging the processing of grievances that should otherwise be heard and may only lead to further conflict, particularly in cases where the remedy is less than sought by the union. If an employee is reinstated without back pay—who is the "losing party"? If the internal dispute procedure fails to serve its intended therapeutic function, the trade-off may hardly be worthwhile.

---

[12]See the Back Pay Act, 5 U.S.C. §5596(b)(1) and 5 U.S.C. §7701(q).

At least one collective bargaining agreement in the federal sector allows the arbitrator to apportion costs depending on the relative merits of the parties' cases. Even in the face of such language, however, arbitrators will rarely go beyond either splitting the costs or charging one party entirely. Indeed, such language could even give rise to an additional hearing to take evidence on how the parties believe the costs should be split. This would bring dispute resolution to the point of absurdity.

Some labor agreements, particularly in the public sector, provide that arbitrators' decisions shall not be binding but, rather, will be considered only as recommendations. Nonbinding decisions are often employed in public sector "fact-finding" cases for resolving so-called "interest" disputes over the terms of a new contract. But a number of states have had marked success with final and binding arbitration in this area.

6

Seniority

Theory

When there is no union representing employees, management has substantial flexibility with respect to assigning jobs and shifts, upgrading, or, indeed, determining which employees to retain or terminate. Prior to the advent of collective bargaining, the employer is the sole and final decider of issues, relying on its own self-interests.

There is no more important aspect to unionization than comprehensive protection of seniority rights. Negotiating demands may include a systematic method for handling employee movement between jobs and shifts, as well as for laying off employees when a temporary or permanent reduction in the need for their services occurs. Unions usually seek to have length of service with the employer adopted as the controlling factor in such moves. In this way, it is reasoned, those working for the employer the longest and who, by their tenure, demonstrated their competence and loyalty to the employer would have preference in various respects over more recently hired employees. These include access to better paying and more highly skilled jobs and jobs on preferred shifts. Senior employees would be entitled to retain present positions with moves to less desirable shifts or positions or even layoff status being thrust initially upon junior or more recently hired employees.

A question that often surfaces is whether seniority alone—pure rank order—will control or whether, instead, the concept of numerical order will be considered together with other factors, such as ability to perform the work. And in this latter context, the question arises as to whether ability alone is sufficient or whether relative ability is at issue. This will be discussed in greater detail.

As a general matter, however, in a case where the potential move involves performance of the same duties, such as might occur in a shift change, seniority may be the sole factor, because the requisite job skills are presumed to have already been proven on the prior shift.

In an upgrading situation, on the other hand, job skills may not be so readily presumed. In such a case, the parties may provide that seniority will prevail only after the skill and ability issue has been settled. There are two major varieties of language to be considered in this context. The first honors seniority, provided the employee seeking to make the move has the basic level of skill and ability required for the sought-after job. For example,

> On promotions seniority will control, provided the employee has the requisite skill and ability.

Most arbitrators will consider this a "threshold" clause, requiring not that the employee be better than less senior candidates but merely that he or she be able to do the work.

In other instances, the parties provide for a "relative" ability test, giving equal or varying weight to the several criteria used to determine qualifications for a move.

> Skill and ability will control in promotions. But if two or more employees have equal skill and ability, then seniority will govern.

Other variations are possible. Language may couple skill and ability as one component with seniority as the other. Such language is subject to interpretation as being a balance so that substantial seniority with minimal skill and ability, for example, could conceivably be weighed against substantial skill and ability with minimal seniority.

Consider the following language:

> Skill, ability, and seniority will be given equal weight in filling promotional positions.

What does this mean? Apparently, the parties wished to "balance" skill and ability against seniority. But how much seniority will outweigh skill? And how does one measure relative degrees of ability, assuming both employees can do the job? Is there a difference between "skill" and "ability"? There are no crystal-clear answers to these questions. This language may properly be regarded as troublesome, indeed.

The following language demonstrates another situation in which the pendulum is weighted in favor of skill and ability and against seniority:

> Seniority shall be an element in addition to skill and ability in the selection of employees for promotion.

The foregoing examples indicate how seemingly minor variations in language may have significant impact. These provisions spawn numerous disputes precisely because the important philosophic underpinnings are often not clearly established by the resulting language. The results are clearly critical. From employees' viewpoints, the tenor of the language could be important to one seeking an opportunity for a promotion to a better paying, more responsible, and more respected position. It could bring promise of a chance to move to a day shift where the employee would be able to enjoy a work schedule permitting more waking hours with children, or it could mean protection against layoff in times of economic recession. It should be noted that there may exist a considerable split within the work force on these points. The more senior group will naturally prefer a strict seniority clause. Younger members may well lean toward "skill and ability" language.

From the employer's viewpoint, variations in language might mean the difference between assigning to an important new position a long-service employee of average performance as against a bright and promising recent hire with specialized training, newly acquired in technical schools or prior employment. It might mean closer supervision and increased costs, therefore, in promoting the average employee in contrast to valued training for the new "hotshot" in preparation for future advancement.

A strict seniority clause does have the virtue of resolving seniority questions easily. The "older" employee wins. As indicated above, much greater difficulty may result in determining whether a particular employee possesses the requisite skill and ability to perform a particular job, and even more difficult is the question of relative skill and ability of two employees competing for the same opening.

There are other issues, too. Questions arise as to whether an employee's skill and ability derived from his present position are relevant as opposed to the skills requisite to performing duties of the position being sought.

—— Case ——

Lorn Early and Don Lately are both operators bidding for the position of lead man. Early has 15 years' seniority compared with Lately's 12, but the latter filled the lead man position for three weeks last summer when Early was on vacation. The contract provides:

> On promotions, seniority shall control if skill and ability are equal.

The Company promoted Lately and Early grieved.

Questions and Comments

(1) *Should the standard be skill and ability on the operator job or on the lead man job?*

Most contracts are vague or silent as to whether the reference to skill and ability refers to that gathered on the current job or that required for the job being sought. Unless there is clear reference to skill and ability to perform the upcoming job, many arbitrators conclude that parties intended the standard to be employed among bidders whose skill and ability have been demonstrated in their current positions. The assumption is that the proficiency level is not only the best basis for comparison but also often the only basis that provides the employer with an adequate gauge as to future performance. While a question sometimes arises in this respect, most arbitrators have held that judgments like this should be made on the assumption that the employee will receive adequate break-in time in the position being sought.

In attempting to resolve ambiguities, the parties may introduce evidence as to the history of their relationship showing contract language changes, the practice in handling skill and ability issues in the past, or perhaps the sequence of proposals and discussions that occurred during one or more prior contract negotiations.

(2) *Should Lately be permitted to prevail just because Early, who should have gotten the temporary assignment, was on vacation?*

Even though Lately did have a prior assignment to the lead man job, such passing access to the higher position would not normally be considered determinative in arbitration. To so hold would place an unwarranted premium on such temporary assignments. In contracts where the employer has the unilateral right to make such temporary upgradings, this could tend to vitiate the whole concept of competitive bidding by stacking the skills in favor of the "preferred" bidder.

But a longer term assignment to the higher position or a former permanent holding of that position might well have provided a bidder with superior skills and ability in the sought-after job. The arbitrator would be obligated to recognize this, and it might result in the superior, albeit junior, candidate being granted the position.

(3) *Would your answer differ if Lately has only one year of seniority?*

Regardless of whether the arbitrator adheres to the standard of skill and ability on the operator job or on the lead man job and regardless of how he or she credits temporary experience on the latter job, the disparity of seniority between two bidders is irrelevant, given this contract language. If one bidder is considered to have greater skill and ability, that employee prevails.

The most troublesome issue in the general area of seniority is determining skill and ability to fill a particular vacancy. The great majority of contracts sets forth skill and ability in those or comparable terms as objective standards.

Thus, the employer chooses a particular employee as meeting the contractual requirements of skill and ability, leaving the union to protest that selection on behalf of one or more individuals whose bids were rejected—presumably because they *lacked* the requisite skill and ability. Such protest takes the form of a grievance which, if unresolved and appealed to arbitration, defers to the arbitrator the determination of whether or not the employer's denial of the position to the grievant was contractually correct. In such a case, the union has the burden of proving that the employer violated the agreement in denying the position to the grievant whom the union claims had the requisite skill and ability.

Sufficient Ability versus Relative Ability

Although contracts often establish objective standards of "ability," comparability among bidders or between the grievant and the individual awarded the position is bound to arise during consideration of such cases. Is the ability called for in the contract a baseline ability to perform the disputed work, or is it the "greatest" ability to perform the disputed work? The former, baseline, "sufficient," or "threshold" ability would require only a showing of minimal ability to do the work on the part of any applicant, resulting in the selection of the most senior among those possessing that baseline ability. The latter, "greatest," or relative ability standard might foreclose reliance on seniority and might grant the employer control on selection, provided it was not arbitrary or capricious. To award the vacancy to the most able would, at best, relegate seniority as a criterion to be used only in the rare instances of breaking ties between two employees with equal ability.

—— Case ——

Jon Haughton and Mike Stutz both bid for the same vacancy. Stutz, who was senior, had filled the job for two months as a temporary transfer. Haughton, who has three years' less service with the company, had done the disputed work for two years with another employer before coming to the company. The company selected Haughton and the senior Stutz grieved. The contract provides: "Promotions shall be based on skill, ability, and seniority."

Questions and Comments

(1) *As arbitrator, what problems would you have with the provision? How would you rule?*

This is a good example of ambiguity in contract language. Does the phrase "skill and ability and seniority" mean that all three are to be given equal weight? Or does it mean skill and ability are to be considered as one element with seniority as the other? Are the two or three elements to be weighed on a balance so that if seniority is the greatest of the three or the greater of the two, the senior employee is to prevail? If the parties offered evidence as to negotiating history of past practice, that might provide necessary guidance to the arbitrator in resolving the contract language consistent with the parties' intent. Most arbitrators would probably consider seniority as merely one element to be considered along with the other two and, in the cited example, could find the junior Haughton to have sufficiently greater skill and ability to prevail over the senior Stutz.

(2) *If the contract read, "In the event of a tie in skill and ability, seniority will govern," how should one rule?*

This language contains a similar ambiguity. Does it mean that seniority prevails in the event "skill" is equal to "ability"? A preferable reading would assume the phrase to mean in the event of a tie "between bidders" in skill and ability, seniority will govern. But does the assumption of those two words mean that the arbitrator is "adding to" or "modifying" the parties' agreement? Most arbitrators would probably find that under the preferred reading of the provision, both had the requisite skill and ability. Here, too, there is a question as to what is meant by "tie." That term would have its true worth if both had filled the job for two months, or if both had equal prior experience. It would be difficult for the arbitrator to precisely weigh the different experiences and he or she might properly rely on the reasonableness of the employer's choice. Or, based upon the parties' prior practice, one might find the application of the term "tie" to have been much less specific, thus finding both had the same skill and ability and granting the grievance.

(3) *What if the contract read, "Seniority shall govern if applicants have the requisite skill and ability"?*

This language would be the easiest for the arbitrator if he or she found that both Stutz and Haughton had the basic skill and ability to do the work, even if one were somewhat better qualified than the other. Assuming the temporary transfer and the pre-employment work showed that both had the necessary skill and ability, the senior Stutz would prevail.

Seniority Units

Relative seniority connotes some basis for the comparison. But what kind of seniority did the parties intend? Does seniority with the company control or seniority in the department? In a multi-unit operation like an automobile manufacturer, should seniority be based on length of service with the company or in the particular plant? In some corporations or governmental units, only certain departments or divisions are organized. Seniority would thus presumably be based on service in that particular bargaining unit.

Hopefully, such questions are resolved in negotiations when the parties secure agreement on the unit to be considered in comparing relative seniority. In a number of enterprises, departmental seniority has had the effect of restricting the upward mobility of minority or female employees whose entry level positions and subsequent chain of positions were confined to certain departments outside the promotional ladder. Thus, white males with a greater breadth of experience were found to have greater prospect of promotion to a wider range of positions, while the departmental seniority offered little advancement prospect to females or minority employees competing with one another for the few advancement opportunities within those dead-end departments. As a consequence of court litigation, departmental seniority systems intended to restrict advancement opportunities because of sex or race have been held illegal.

Nonetheless many contracts still have clauses providing for departmental seniority.[1] A female or minority bidder may claim in arbitration that the departmental seniority provision is an illegal bar to the grievant's legitimate claim for advancement. However, most arbitrators will adhere to their traditional role of interpreting the contract as written, leaving to the parties their inherent right to challenge the legality of the provision through the courts or administrative agencies.

Mergers of Seniority Lists

The objective of the merger is usually to integrate the lists from the former enterprises into one new list with minimal dislocation to either group. The easiest procedure is to integrate seniority strictly according to date of hire in either of the merging enterprises. If the resultant merger of an older with a newer firm is expected to result in some reduction of personnel, the integration of one list composed chiefly of junior employees with the other list having mostly senior employees would place the whole burden of any cutback on the junior employees. This would be particularly objectionable, of course, if it was the junior enterprise that took over the senior enterprise—hardly a situation in which the purchasing firm would be expected to have its employees suffer from the move.

In addition to the strict date-of-hire approach, there are other devices for merging diverse seniority units. One is a weighted seniority scale in which employees of a junior unit are

---

[1]See *Teamsters v. United States*, 431 U.S. 324 (1977), wherein the Supreme Court held that Section 703(h) of Title VII of the 1964 Civil Rights Act protects a bona fide seniority system, even though it perpetuates pre-Act unintentional discrimination.

See also *American Tobacco Co. et al v. Patterson et al*, 456 U.S. 63 (1982). There, the Supreme Court held that Section 703(h) is not limited to seniority systems adopted before the effective date of the Act. To construe it as so limited, the Court held, would be contrary to the plain language of Section 703(h), inconsistent with prior cases, and contrary to national labor policy.

given weighted seniority dates to achieve a better spread of these fewer people in the larger seniority grouping, adding the necessary number of years to their seniority to make their dates more comparable to employees in the other unit.

Another procedure used when there is to be a merger of large and small units, i.e., one four times the size of the other, is to provide a ratio system wherein, for example, one slot for the most senior person from the smaller unit is established after every four slots in the larger unit. The parties also frequently negotiate other devices for achieving such integration relying on skills, age, qualification test scores, or certifications to weigh some employees differently than others and to thus overcome adherence to strict seniority.

Professor Tom Kennedy indicated criteria for such integration in a paper before the National Academy of Arbitrators.[2] Kennedy identified five methods: (1) the *surviving group principle*, whereby lists are merged by adding the names of the employees of the acquired company to the bottom of the list of the acquiring company; (2) the *length of service principle*, where the list treats all employees as if they had always been employed by the same company or plant using a straight length of service criteria; (3) the *follow the work principle*, where employees are given the opportunity to follow their work (if it can still be identified) with seniority rights to such work; if the work cannot be identified, the lists are integrated into a single list on a ratio basis representing the amount of work brought to the consolidation by each group of employees; (4) the *absolute rank principle*, which places employees on the merged list on the basis of the rank they held on their respective prior lists; and (5) the *ratio rank principle*, which requires establishing a ratio from the number of employees in each of the groups to be merged and assigning places on the new list according to the ratio.

Broken Seniority

If seniority is based upon date of entry into the seniority unit, it would seem logical that it would terminate on the date of

---

[2]See Kennedy, "Merging Seniority Lists," in *Labor Arbitration and Industrial Change*, Proceedings of the 16th Annual Meeting, National Academy of Arbitrators (Washington, D.C.: BNA Books, 1963), at 1; see also Elkouri & Elkouri, *How Arbitration Works* (Washington, D.C.: BNA Books, 3rd ed. 1973), at 564–567.

departure from that unit. In most situations, that is true. But the parties may negotiate exceptions to that rule for anticipated situations where individuals leave the bargaining unit with the expectation of returning.

For example, leaves of absence for health reasons, child rearing, military duty, or Peace Corps service are often foreseen by the negotiators. This may result in seniority protections for those involved. In addition, the contract may protect rights of employees who leave their regular tasks to take an assignment in a non-union portion of the employer's operation or in management, although contracts will differ as to whether seniority continues to accrue during such leaves, as noted below. The contract may specify a time limit during which seniority will be protected. After that, if the employee had not returned to the bargaining unit, his or her seniority rights would be cancelled and return to the bargaining unit would be as a new employee. The same arrangement may be constructed to protect seniority rights of employees when they opt to take temporary or even permanent positions with their unions. Other labor agreements provide for the effective vesting of any earned seniority.

When the parties negotiate break-in-seniority provisions, they usually address the question of whether seniority continues to accrue during the break or whether it is frozen. If the latter option is agreed to, then an employee with six years' seniority, when leaving the bargaining unit, will, on return two years later, have a simulated hiring date two years less than the date on which the individual was actually hired.

──── **Case** ────

Mary Clark had 12 years' seniority in the bargaining unit when she was offered a full-time position with Union A. After six months in that role, she left that union to go to work for Union B. After two months, when that proved uncomfortable, she sought to return to her old bargaining-unit position, but the company refused and Union A grieved. The contract provision in question reads:

An employee who goes into management or to work for the union will retain seniority for three years.

Questions and Comments

(1) *If you were the arbitrator, how would you rule?*

It could be argued that the purpose of the disputed provision was to protect seniority of employees when they departed the bargaining unit for short-term assignments, regardless of whether they went to work for management or unions and regardless of which enterprise or which union. It could also be argued that the parties' specific intent was to credit such absences only when their organizations themselves were to be the beneficiaries of the time away from the bargaining unit. Therefore, the coverage of the language should not be extended to employment by another union.

A narrower interpretation of the provision would rely on the phrase "the union" as referring to only the union that negotiated the agreement, and thus probably bar preservation of seniority while employed by the second union.

(2) *What if Clark had gone into this company's management from Union A instead of to the rival union?*

In the preceding question the answer would probably be founded on the language of the parties' agreement as declaring an intent to permit outside work either for the management of that company or the union (A) of its employees. The same strict construction could be involved in this fact situation as well. But here, the facts cover employment by both signatory parties, within the prescribed three years, although the contract says "or" not "both." Although the option of working for "both" is not specified in the agreement, it would probably be found to be within the parties' intent in agreeing to the provision, particularly when the total time span is within that agreed to. A different result might be expected if the employment by each party were for a two-year period, thus for "both" exceeding the three-year limit agreed to.

(3) *If she had the right to return, what would be the result if employees with her seniority were on layoff?*

Even assuming the agreement sets forth a right of return to work, that right is not absolute. It arises from the parties' intent to preserve grievant's seniority. It would therefore follow that the employee who took advantage of that provision should be accorded the same treatment vis-à-vis seniority as though he or she had continued at work throughout this period and not taken such leave. If that course had resulted in a layoff, the employee who opted for the management and/or union stint would thus, in effect, return to layoff status.

But what if the leave ran past the three-year period during which seniority is retained and when return to the bargaining unit would have resulted in the employee's layoff? Would the next junior employee on layoff at the end of the three-year leave period have a valid claim for moving up one notch on the layoff list? If a laid-off employee is entitled to secure alternative employment during layoff, should not the employee on the union/management leave be entitled to remain in his or her interim leave position beyond the three-year limit to avoid return to the bargaining unit and thus layoff? Or would refusal to return to layoff status after three years jeopardize seniority?

Same or Comparable Job

In determining reinstatement rights of an employee returning to the bargaining unit, a question may arise as to whether the grievant is entitled to return to the same job as held before, or whether the employer is obligated only to return the grievant to its employ or to the same *classification* as held before. This, too, is a question that should be addressed by the parties in negotiations. Where the contract is silent on this subject, the arbitrator may be required to resolve the issue based on the language the parties *did* agree to.

—— **Case** ——

Joshua Spar sought to return to his former bargaining unit as Machine Operator LG5 after a period of time working as a foreman. The company said it was not required by the contract to place him in the machine operator position so long as his rate was protected. The employee grieved. The contract provides:

> An employee returning to the bargaining unit after no more than one year of service in management shall be reinstated in his former classification.

Questions and Comments

(1) *As an arbitrator, how would you rule? Does the employer have the right to assign Spar to an operator assistant position in LG3 though it pays him the LG5 rate?*

Arbitrators have held that when the parties negotiate language such as this they agree to permit employees taking such leave to return to their former classification. They did not agree to return employees to their particular machines, shifts, or departments. But by having selected the term "classification" it must be assumed that the parties meant to have such employees return to the work they had been doing before. Although the pay for the job is certainly an important justification for wanting to return to one's same classification, the parties did not agree that on return an employee would merely be pay-protected. They agreed to return to classification, even if it is occupied at the time of return, and the returning employee is entitled to be re-established in that position, consistent with seniority. With a job come certain benefits beyond compensation, including greater skill development and greater access to promotion, which should be observed under the language in question.

(2) *What if the position were abolished in the interim?*

A different result would obtain if the disputed classification had been abolished. If such were the case, the employee would be entitled to that placement he would have reached had he not left for the management position. Some arbitrators would conclude that the grievant is entitled to pay protection in such a situation, but most would hold that the employee is entitled to no greater protection than would have been granted had he stayed in his classification until its abolition.

(3) *Assuming the company could place him in LG3, because no vacancy exists in LG5, would he have an automatic right to go to LG5 if it became vacant?*

If the contract provided the employer the right to return the employee to a lower labor grade with pay protection, it should follow that so long as full compensation is received, the employee's rights are limited to those that would flow to an occupant of that LG3 position. Arbitrators might differ as to the employee's right to move into the LG5 position, some taking the position that normal bidding procedures be followed. The larger number might hold that the return to LG3 was only in lieu of a vacancy in LG5 and move the employee into the LG5 opening forthwith.

Superseniority

Management's exercise of its right to assign, promote, and lay off employees, even if implemented in conformity with the contractual protections for seniority, is bound to result in occasional movement or assignment of union officers or shop stewards. If this occurs, employees remaining in a department or a shift might be deprived of a readily available union official to assist them in dealings with management, handling grievances, and the like. In a plant where the union officers are among the junior employees, for instance, a substantial layoff could effectively eliminate union representation for the remaining employees.

To protect against this possibility, and to ensure that management, too, has a union representative on tap to communicate with in the event of a dispute, parties often negotiate special language, referred to as "superseniority" clauses. These clauses provide exceptions to the general rules of seniority and assure that a specified number of union officials will be exempted from layoffs, etc., to remain available to service members in the particular department, shift, or plant.

Thus, the agreement might provide that at least one shop steward or other union officer would remain per shift and/or per department in event of a layoff, or that a shop steward would be given priority in movement to any shift or department from which a union representative had been laid off or bumped.

——— Case ———

Janie Lewis was shop steward in Department 5 night shift prior to a period of layoff. When a vacancy occurred in the day shift, she applied for it. The company admitted she had the requisite seniority, but assigned William Shaw, a junior employee, on the ground that to move Lewis would deprive the night shift, when it returns to work, of any union officers.

The pertinent contract provision reads as follows:

> The union shall have the right to retain a union shop steward on each shift, in the event of a reduction in force.

Question and Comment

(1) *If you were the arbitrator, how would you rule?*

Although the company may be correct in assessing the deprivation of union representation that would result from the movement of Lewis from the night shift to the day shift, it may not be within its province to assert a right of union representation for the employees. If the contract language had stated "there shall be a union representative on each shift," the employer might argue that it was within its authority in insisting that Lewis remain on the night shift. Even then, however, most arbitrators would conclude that the individual's right to bid should prevail. The union's right to select another representative is, after all, unaffected. Here, the contract language describes a *union* right to retain a union shop steward on each shift. That phraseology extends to the union, not the employer, the option of determining whether it wishes such shift representation. If the union waives its right to have representation on the night shift, Lewis presumably would have the right to bid on the day shift without company interference.

Loss of Seniority

In addition to language protecting seniority, the parties also frequently negotiate language whereby occurrence of specific events will trigger immediate loss of seniority. These provisions identify situations in which employment itself is to be terminated, since the total elimination of seniority in effect removes the employee from the employer's personnel roster or at least reduces the employee's status to that of a new hire. Consider the following language:

> An employee's seniority with the company will be terminated by any of the following events:
>
> (1) Discharge for just cause,
> (2) Failure to return to work from layoff within 48 hours of recall,
> (3) Absence for more than 48 hours without a reasonable excuse,
> (4) Failure to be recalled from layoff for 12 months, or
> (5) Resignation.

Note that, with the exception of discharge for just cause, the other events refer to situations wherein the individual's seniority is "terminated." Some parties use the term "forfeited" in this context. This is often referred to as a "contractual termination," as opposed to a discharge. The distinction is that there need be no showing of just cause in such instances. Rather, the employee is deemed to have voluntarily quit the employment. This has several implications. For example, in an arbitration involving "absence for more than 48 hours without a reasonable excuse" (No. 3 in the above example), the employer will be justified in taking action merely upon a showing that the employee was absent for more than 48 hours. It is the employee's burden to show there was a good reason. This reverses the normal burden of proof in a discharge case. If the employee had no good reason, the termination stands. Questions of progressive discipline in that context are often found to be inapplicable.

Promotions and Bidding

Issues of skill and ability versus seniority usually arise in the context of lateral transfers or promotions. Vacancies may occur as a result of death, retirement, termination, or promotion of the incumbent.

The parties usually negotiate a procedure of posting vacancies at a known location, such as a prominent bulletin board. The employer posts a job opening with a description of the position, a listing of the qualifications, or both. The notice sets forth a deadline for applying with a designated representative of the employer. Once that deadline is passed, the employer may weigh the relative skill, ability, and seniority of the applicants (depending on the seniority clause) to determine which individual is entitled to fill the vacant position. If there are no qualified applicants, the employer may normally repost the position or hire from the street. Some contracts specify the employer's option to decide if the open position is to be filled. But even without such language, this right is normally inferred. If the contract has objective standards of skill and ability, the employer's conclusion that the applicants lack the requisite skill and ability may be subject to challenge through the grievance and arbitration system.

—— Case ——

A vacancy occurs in the position of lead operator which the company posts for one week as required by contract. No one bids for the position and the company hires a new employee to fill it.

Questions and Comments

(1) *Would a vacationing employee who did not return until after the posting was taken down have a valid grievance?*

The contract provision governing posting is the controlling factor in determining whether an employee on vacation has a right to bid a position posted during his absence. Posting provisions are usually for a set number of days, because of the recognized need of the employer to fill such vacancies as expeditiously as possible. It must be assumed that such language was drafted with recognition that when any particular vacancy was posted some employees would be absent due to illness, jury duty, National Guard duty, vacation, maternity leave, and the like. It would generally be held to be the union's responsibility to make special provision for such absentees. Having failed to do so, most arbitrators would hold that a vacationing employee had no right to unilaterally have the contractual posting period extended until his return.

(2) *If there were two bidders, one with 10 years', the other with 2 years' seniority, under what circumstances would the employer have the right to reject both as lacking skill and ability and instead hire from the street?*

Except in agreements where there is a provision mandating minimum crew size, the employer is usually recognized as having the right to determine if a vacant position is to be filled. Related thereto is the right to determine whether bidders for a posted vacancy possess the requisite skills to master the open position. Since the contract usually contains the criteria of skill and ability, the employer's judgment on that score is subject to challenge through the grievance procedure. Although the test of skill and ability on the bidder's present position is the usual standard, one is justified in requiring some demonstrable evidence that such skills are somehow meaningful to the job at issue. The union, as the moving party, has the burden of establishing that one or more of the bidders meet the objective criteria, and the arbitrator has to determine whether the employer acted reasonably in holding that none possessed the requisite skill and ability. Among the factors that might be raised by the employer in defense of the right to hire outside instead of promoting one of the bidders might be (1) certification or license requirements mandated for the lead operator position that bidders lacked, (2) a poor attendance or tardiness record when the open position requires constant, reliable attendance throughout every workday, (3) a prior skill and ability record which, although excellent, would be totally unrelated to the complex machinery and high-level skills of the vacant position, and (4) a record of consistent overtime refusal when the open position reasonably demands a healthy measure of overtime availability.

Even though a bidder may never have filled the sought-after job, it is appropriate to examine performance in the positions the applicant has filled. Depending on the arbitrator, a record of commendations and evidence of superior output or of willingness to work extra hours may all be considered as factors favoring an applicant. To the contrary, evidence of warnings as to poor workmanship, a poor attendance record, or of consistent unwillingness to work overtime may be considered as adverse factors that might properly exclude an employee from consideration. Likewise, if a prior position contained some of the same elements as the position being sought, ability to adequately perform the related job elements might be crucial evidence of ability to perform the same aspects in the vacant job.

(3) *If the contract called for a 10-day posting period and a grievance was filed by Jack Wright, who wished to bid but had been out sick until the ninth day, would the fact that the company had already hired someone for the slot dispose of the case? If not, to what remedy would grievant be entitled?*

Just as the vacationing employee has no unilateral right to extend the posting period, the employer may not unilaterally shorten it. If the contract called for a 10-day posting, the employer acted at its peril in filling that position prior to the end of that period, whether promoting from within or hiring from the outside. If Wright submitted a bid on his return from his illness, he would be entitled to consideration pursuant to the promotion standards, provided his bid was submitted prior to the contractual posting deadline. Then, if he prevailed on the merits, the person who was prematurely placed in the vacancy would have to be removed. If he merely complained on his return that his bid time should be extended, his grievance would lack merit. He was obligated to file his bid by the deadline.

Written or Oral Tests

Employers sometimes seek to avoid conflict or to eliminate their own uncertainty over whether or not an employee has the requisite abilities by subjecting employees to written or oral tests designed to establish qualifications for a particular job or group of jobs. To the extent the employer's selection is based upon the test results alone, such a device may overcome the challenge of arbitrariness in the employer's determination of who is fit and able to fill a vacancy. There is a growing body of law, however, in which tests have been carefully scrutinized as to potential discriminatory impact against minority employees.

For a test to objectively establish qualification, it must be related to the job being filled, fair, reasonable, and fairly administered. Failure to meet any one of these criteria may be grounds for disregarding the test results as the controlling factor for ascertaining skill and ability.

If the test does meet the above standards, an employee may be obligated to take such a test in order to qualify for consideration for a position. Refusal to do so might be considered a waiver of the employee's right to challenge the propriety of the test or at least a waiver of his right to fill the vacancy.

 Case

Joe Jackson, who had filled the vacant job routinely on a temporary basis, received a score of 72 on his only try at a skill test for the job. Peter Schwab, who had never filled the post, even on a temporary basis, flunked the test twice, but got a 76 on his third try. Schwab was awarded the job. Jackson grieved.

Questions and Comments

(1) *Was the third test valid if it had been given twice before to Schwab?*

Tests as an element of the promotion process may be a subject of negotiations. If they are, questions, such as the number of times they may be taken, are usually a matter of negotiation. But if the test is unilaterally introduced by the employer as an aid in its determination of, say, skill and ability, the test scores have validity only as evidence to support the employer's contention that its selection of Schwab was correct. In the latter situation, Schwab had taken the test three times and perhaps learned sufficient answers in the process to achieve a higher score. That fact might be considered by the arbitrator as reducing the contribution of the test score to the employer's determination.

(2) *Would it be fair to Jackson to base the selection on the test if, as a black, he claimed a lack of prior exposure to such tests or that the test questions were discriminatory?*

Most arbitrators follow the precept that the basis of their authority is the contract rather than the law. Thus, in a case in which the legal validity of such tests is brought into question, most would confine themselves to the questions raised within the contract. In so doing, they might note in their opinion that the question as to the legal validity of such tests is a matter for the courts to resolve rather than the arbitrator. A minority of arbitrators (see Chapter 3) embrace the rulings of courts in making their judgments on the contract. They might rule on both legal and contractual questions in the cited examples.[3]

-----

[3] See *Gulf States Utilities,* 62 LA 1061 (Williams, 1974), where the arbitrator decided the employer properly demoted the black employee who failed the test even though the test would be considered racially discriminatory under EEOC guidelines. See also *Industrial Garment Mfg. Co.,* 74 LA 1248 (Griffin, 1980), where the arbitrator found the employer did not violate the contract by discriminating against employees by requiring a test in lieu of a high school education. In *ASG Industries Inc.,* 62 LA 849 (1974), Arbitrator Foster found the employer did not violate the contract when it eliminated a general aptitude test to avoid racial discrimination, since the employer believed the test could not pass EEOC guidelines. In *Joy Mfg. Co., Robbins Div.,* 70 LA 4 (1970), Arbitrator Matthews found that the employer acted properly when it failed to award an assembler

Trial Period

A decision by management that an employee who has never filled a position has the fitness and ability to perform a particular job is subject to the risk of being disproven. To protect the employer against forced retention of an employee in a position for which he or she is not deemed suited, contracts often provide a reasonable trial period. The trial period is also a benefit to the employee, who may have a reasonable time to become acquainted with the position. Frequently, the employee will have the option of returning to his former post if the trial is unsuccessful or, in some cases, if the new position is not to his liking.

Often, however, an employee will view the trial period as an opportunity for achieving qualifications that may have been lacking in the employee's background prior to the time of application. Whether the trial period is interpreted as providing this final opportunity for training is a matter depending upon careful contract construction. Absent language suggesting the "trial period" is meant for training, most arbitrators will not infer such right.

------ **Case** ------

Steven Rivo, the senior employee, was bypassed in favor of a junior employee in filling a vacancy in the position of operator. Alison Dasher, the junior employee, had substantial experience in doing the main functions of the vacant job.

---

job to a black man who scored only 25 percent on a blueprint reading test, despite the fact the contract required all job classifications to remain open to everyone.

In *Griggs v. Duke Power Co.*, 401 U.S. 424 (1971), the Supreme Court stated: "Nothing in the [1964 Civil Rights] Act precludes the use of testing or measuring procedures [so long as the tests] measure the person for the job and not the person in the abstract."

Lower courts that have considered a challenge to a test brought under the Civil Rights Act of 1964 (see 2002(e) (2)) have required a demonstration that the testing has resulted in a disproportionate impact on the minority's ability to secure promotion before the courts will consider questions as to the validity of the tests. *Moore v. Southwestern Bell Tel. Co.*, 593 F. 2d 517 (5 Cir. 1976); *Blake v. Los Angeles*, 435 F. Supp. 55 (C.D. Cal. 1977), *rev'd on other grounds*, 595 F. 2d 1367 (9th Cir. 1978).

The parties' agreement reads as follows:

A 30-day break-in period shall be provided for employees selected to fill job vacancies.

Rivo filed a grievance, demanding a 30-day opportunity to prove himself in the open position.

Questions and Comments

(1) *As arbitrator, how would you rule?*

The break-in period normally is not intended as part of the training period to establish requisite skill and ability an applicant is expected to have at the time of bidding. Rather, as the term implies, the break-in period is intended to provide an opportunity for the employee, once selected for the new position, to adapt his earlier experience to the demands of the new job. Thus, if Rivo, the senior bidder, lacked the requisite skill and ability at the time of bidding, he has no standing after the selection of the then-more-qualified Dasher, the junior employee, to demand access to the break-in period. The break-in period is the unique entitlement of the successful bidder.

(2) *Under the provision, does the junior employee have a right to move back to her former position if she decides she does not like the job?*

If Dasher, the successful bidder, decided she did not like the new position during the break-in period, the consensus is that, absent break-in language to the contrary, she would have the right to bid back to her former position. The break-in period is generally considered a two-way street with either the employer or the employee entitled to back out of the new arrangement if either one reasonably believes it to be unacceptable.

(3) *If the junior employee abandons the position and Rivo was the only other bidder, would he get the job?*

If Dasher opts to return to her former position, Rivo would be entitled to move into the vacancy only if he met the requirements of skill and ability as set forth in the contract. If he did not, then the employer would have the options of leaving the position vacant, re-opening it for new bids, or going outside to hire a new employee therefor.

(4) *If the company finds after three days that the junior employee cannot handle the job, must it nevertheless allow her to complete the full 30-day period?*

No one would expect an employer to tolerate for the full 30-day break-in period a successful bidder who cut such a swath of destruction that all could see she would never succeed in the job. But in most cases, arbitrators would seek to provide the newly promoted person more than three days to overcome the trauma associated with breaking-in on a new job. That the parties agreed to a 30-day break-in period is usually persuasive evidence that they recognized that no new employee would become an immediate master of the new position, and that a 30-day period is required for a fair evaluation of the employee's ability to fulfill the demands thereof.

Layoff

If business conditions dictate, and unless otherwise proscribed by contract, the employer has the right to reduce its manpower. It must do so in conformity with the requirements of the parties' bargaining agreement. Sometimes the parties may agree to forestall layoffs by reducing the work week for the entire work force below the normal 40-hour week instead of laying off a percentage of the employees. Whether this is permitted depends, again, on the parties' agreement.

A number of restrictions on management's otherwise unfettered right to reduce manpower may be written into the parties' contract. There may be a requirement of timely notice of the reduction. There will probably be language establishing a layoff status, as distinguished from termination, granting laid-off employees a right to recall if employment should again pick up. The normal practice is to follow a "last-out first-in" system of recall based upon seniority standing. If recall does not occur

within the layoff period established by contract, the employment status of the laid-off employees would evolve to termination and they would be removed from the company roster.

Bumping

Bumping questions arise when fewer than all employees
are laid off. Here seniority plays a crucial role. Most collective
bargaining agreements contain language permitting senior employees to retain their positions with the brunt of the layoff being borne by the junior employees.

In a cutback, superfluous jobs are not held by only the most
junior employees. As a consequence, the concept of bumping
has developed. Under that process, if the position of a senior
employee is declared surplus, the occupant of that position has
the right, in lieu of layoff, to move into a still-functioning position held by a less senior employee. That individual, in turn, has
the right to bump an even less senior employee, and so on until,
when there is no one else to bump, the junior employees are actually laid off.

Labor agreements set forth this bumping right as well as
restrictions thereon requiring that the senior employee have
the ability to perform the tasks of the position into which he or
she is bumping. In some cases, the agreement restricts bumping
rights to those positions previously occupied by the senior
employee.

 Case ——

Article 5 of the parties' agreement permits the
employer to make a temporary assignment of employees for up to 30 days.

Article 6 provides that, in the event of a layoff, an
employee has the right to bump into any position where
he or she can do the job, in lieu of layoff. On October 7,
the company announces a layoff to begin October 14.
The same day, it informs machinist 1st class Sharon
Bonin that it is temporarily transferring her to machin-

ist helper. Bonin grieves, claiming she is entitled to bump into machinist 2nd class during layoff.

Questions and Comments

(1) *Which provision controls? For how long?*

Since the company action in moving Bonin to machinist helper occurred one week prior to the effective date of the layoff, it would appear that Article 5 would control since there was, as yet, no layoff. Between October 7 and 14, Bonin would be in the temporary assignment and Article 5 would control. Most temporary transfers to lower paying jobs provide for income protection for the duration of the assignment, while bumps usually call for payment of the rate for the classification into which bumped. Thus, Bonin would probably be better off financially than if she bumped into machinist 2nd class. Presumably she would have the skill to fill both lower classifications. If the employer opted to save the difference in salary, it would probably be within its rights in cutting short the temporary assignment on October 14, then justifying Bonin's bump into the lower paying slot.

Under the layoff provision, Article 6, Bonin would probably not have the option of cutting short the temporary assignment in favor of the bump into the machinist 2nd class slot since she was properly transferred under Article 5, and could only invoke her Article 6 bumping rights when the alternative would be actual layoff. Her alternative under the facts would presumably be to remain in the helper classification rather than suffer the layoff.

(2) *If Bonin bumped into the 2nd class machinist, could she later bump a junior 1st class machinist?*

Since the contract provision specifies that a bumping employee must be able to perform the duties of the classification into which he or she is bumping, Bonin, having formerly been a machinist 1st class, would be entitled to bump a junior 1st class machinist later. But if Bonin had never been a 1st class machinist, she could only bump into the 1st class classification if she were able to demonstrate to the satisfaction of the employer, or perhaps the arbitrator, that she could perform 1st class duties.

(3) *If Bonin wanted to bump into a position she had never held before, would she be entitled to a break-in period to prove her ability?*

If Bonin desired to bump into a position never before occupied, she would be governed by the contractual requirement of ability to do that job. Any break-in provision found elsewhere in the agreement would have no applicability in such a move. The ability to handle the job must precede the bump, rather than evolve during the break-in period.

Recall

The general standard of "last-out first-in," when applied to recalls, grants the senior laid-off employees priority on returning to active, full-time employment. Generally, the employer is required to provide reasonable notice of recall to an employee, and the employee in turn is required to report to work by the time specified.

Remedies

If an employee is successful in grieving improper treatment under the seniority provisions of the parties' agreement, he or she is entitled to a remedy to rectify the error. To the extent that the error by management resulted in layoff instead of being permitted to bump a junior employee, the employee is entitled to reimbursement of money otherwise earned, had there been permission to fill the junior position. To the extent the employee was not properly recalled from layoff to re-employment, he or she is likewise entitled to compensation for earnings lost.

Computation of earnings lost may run beyond the loss of the actual straight-time earnings of the position denied, so that reimbursement for overtime work, which might reasonably have been received had the assignment been properly made as well as entitlement to vacation pay, holiday pay, and the like, may be included. In some cases, a premature layoff would entitle the employee to those earnings only for the period until they would properly have been laid off.

A more difficult problem arises in correcting the improper placement of the employee where, for example, achieving contract compliance may well be the displacement of another employee. This may create political problems for the company or the union that might better be resolved by a negotiated settlement. But when resolved by the arbitrator, such issues dictate that the letter of the contract be complied with if only to avoid another grievance or a charge that the arbitrator has ignored or rewritten the parties' agreement.

—— **Case** ——

Steve Paley successfully grieved his improper layoff and is entitled to reinstatement to the lower position of operator class B. The junior employee currently holding that position threatens to sue the company and the union if he is removed from it.

Questions and Comments

(1) *If this information is introduced at the hearing, what impact would it have on the remedy to be provided to Paley?*

As noted earlier, the responsibility of the arbitrator is to interpret and apply the contract and, in remedy questions, to make the employee whole for the error committed. The fact that the consequence thereof may result in a lawsuit should have no bearing on the arbitrator's determination that the grievant is entitled to displace an employee wrongly assigned to a position to which he or she was not entitled.

(2) *If Paley is reinstated, would the junior employee be able to grieve his displacement? What if he could prove he was a better operator class B than Paley?*

The junior employee would have the requisite standing to grieve, but the determinations having already been made that Paley's displacement of the junior employee was proper, the grievance would have little prospect of success. Even were he able to prove he was a better operator than Paley, the standard for job filling in layoff and recall normally does not leave room for determination as to who is a better, or more qualified, operator, so long as the senior individual can do the work.

7

Contractual Aspects of Discipline

Disciplinary events under the collective bargaining agreement, as will be noted, flow from managements's express and implied rights to discharge as well as the concomitant obligation to do so for just cause. Before examining those important and diverse issues, however, it is appropriate to distinguish disciplinary situations from the variety of terminations that arise in non-disciplinary contexts. Disputes often occur in cases where employees are terminated for contractual violations that do not involve questions of just cause. For example, labor agreements often provide that the employment relationship will cease in situations having nothing to do with discipline. An agreement might include the following provisions:

Employees' seniority shall cease in the following situations:

(1) An employee has been laid off without being recalled to work for a period of two years.
(2) An employee quits.
(3) An employee fails to return to work within five days following a vacation, suspension, or notice of recall without notifying management he will be absent or, in the alternative, without later supplying satisfactory explanation for the failure to report or call in.

Example 3 is often referred to as a "five-day pull" or "intentional forfeiture of seniority." The contractual presumption is that the employee intended to forfeit the job. While the employer has removed the employee from the rolls, this is properly regarded as a contractual question. Assuming the employee has not, in fact, shown up, the initial presumption is that the employer was justified in terminating him. It is not the employer's burden to demonstrate just cause under those circumstances. Rather, it is the employee's obligation to demonstrate that the employer violated the contract in severing the employment. In arbitration, once the employer has successfully demonstrated, by evidence or by stipulation, that the employee was not at work and that he did not call in, it has satisfied its burden.

—— Case ——

Mark Dickerson called in to his company on January 3 and said he was ill, and that he would return on January 10. However, he did not return on January 10. Management heard nothing from the employee and, on January 16, it removed him from the employment rolls. The labor agreement provided that an employee's seniority shall cease, among other things, where:

an employee fails to return to work within five days following an expected date of return.

Upon his return, he found he had been terminated, but offered to show that he had, in fact, been under medical treatment at all times. The supervisor asked for some medical verification, but grievant said he had left the materials at home. Two weeks later, grievant's union representative presented a mimeographed form stating as follows:

M. *Dickerson* has been under the care of this office from *January 2* to *January 15*. He was treated for *lower back strain*.
s/F. Raud, M.D.

The company rejected the proffered slip and the matter went to arbitration.

Questions and Comments

(1) *Where does the burden of proof lie in this instance?*

While there may be questions as to grievant's veracity, this is a termination case wherein the company contends he forfeited his seniority by failing to report in a timely fashion. Once it is acknowledged that grievant did not report within the requisite five days, it is grievant's burden to show cause as to why the termination should not stand. Note that the labor agreement makes no provision for his supplying a defensible reason. Nevertheless, most arbitrators would refuse to apply the termination if, in fact, it was impossible for the grievant to comply with the reporting requirement. At the same time, the arbitrator would invariably wish to know why, assuming grievant was, in fact, incapacitated, he could not have called the company. A surprisingly large number of cases arise as a result of the lack of such notification.

(2) *What sort of evidence would be demanded of the grievant in such circumstances?*

There is a great deal of misunderstanding with respect to doctors' slips. Often referred to as "$5 (perhaps $25 in these times) slips," the suggestion is that the doctor's attestation can be purchasd without grievant's having truly been incapacitated. Whether the arbitrator draws such inference depends on the nature of the evidence. A mere written attestation will not necessarily suffice, particularly where, as here, there is a suggestion that the evidence was obtained after the illness. The slip itself does not provide strong evidence in the grievant's case. Under the circumstances, arbitrators have concluded that grievant failed to sustain his burden. But what if the doctor were to appear and testify, convincingly, that grievant had been hospitalized for severe lower back problems and that contact with the employer was, for one reason or another, impossible? Practically speaking, one may hardly fault a supervisor, under the circumstances discussed earlier, from concluding that grievant's termination should stand. At the time grievant returned, he presented virtually no reason for the company to act otherwise. At the same time, the fact is that he was truly unable to work. Assuming the company had been informed of this reality, he should not have been terminated. The ultimate question in such a case is not whether the company acted reasonably under the circumstances, but whether it was right. In cases such as this, many arbitrators have held that, while the termination was improper, inasmuch as grievant was, in fact, unable to report during those days, grievant should share the burden of the ensuing dispute for having failed to make the type of showing that would have led to an earlier reinstatement.

Other nondisciplinary but nevertheless adverse actions arise in certain promotion and demotion cases. The management rights clause of a labor agreement may well read as follows:

> Management retains the right to hire, discipline, or discharge for just cause, promote, demote, and manage the work force.

It is generally accepted that "just cause," as it has evolved in the field of discipline and discharge, is inapplicable in the context of decisions to promote or demote. (For purposes of this discussion, one assumes there is no seniority bidding procedure in effect.) In theory, then, management's discretion is unfettered by the standards employed in the disciplinary context. This theory is reflected in numerous arbitration awards concluding that "so long as the decision is free from arbitrary, capricious, or discriminatory motives," the arbitrator will not substitute his or her judgment for that of management.

In practice, the distinction between discipline and a managerial judgment on performance is often significant. With respect to promotions and demotions, management may well be required to show not necessarily that the decision was right but that it was rendered as a normal business judgment in good faith.

This is not to say that good faith alone will always suffice. At some point, the "pure-hearted but empty-headed" administrator will have been found to have made a decision so wholly lacking in foundation as to be construed as capricious and subject to reversal. In discipline cases, on the other hand, an arbitrator will be more willing to require that the decision be correct; the arbitrator will, therefore, more readily substitute his or her judgment for that of management not only as to whether the offense was committed but also as to the extent of appropriate discipline.

Disciplinary Events

The ability to impose discipline and discharge is widely, perhaps universally, regarded as an inherent management right. Omission of any reference to that right in a given contract, therefore, will rarely, if ever, be construed as an intention by the parties to restrict management's right to require proper conduct and performance and to take responsive action in cases of observed lapses. This is consistent with the theory of retained management rights, in which the employer is considered to be restricted only to the extent the labor agreement so provides.[1]

This does not mean, however, that, absent a negotiated standard of reasonableness in imposing such discipline or discharge, management is wholly unrestricted with respect to its disciplinary prerogatives. Most arbitrators will require the employer to provide a reasoned ground for disciplinary action, which has evolved as a standard of "just cause." it is unlikely, therefore, that the absence or presence of a just cause provision will have any demonstrable impact on an arbitrator's view of management's rights and responsibilities in this area.

Indeed, so basic is the inherent assumption of a just cause requirement that parties must specifically provide if such is not to be the case. Such language arises frequently in a number of

---

[1]Note that this discussion concerns employee rights in the context of an organized work force. As Professor Theodore J. St. Antoine of the University of Michigan has noted, the concept of protection against unjust discipline for non-union workers, while embraced by academics and arbitrators for some time, has only recently begun to be adopted by the courts. See "Protection Against Unjust Discipline: An Idea Whose Time Has Long Since Come," in *Arbitration Issues for the 1980s*, Proceedings of the 34th Annual Meeting, National Academy of Arbitrators (Washington, D.C.: BNA Books, 1982), at 43. See also *Monge v. Beebe Rubber Co.*, 114 N.H. 130, 316 A.2d 549 (1974); *Toussaint v. Blue Cross and Blue Shield of Michigan and Ebling v. Masco Corp.*, 408 Mich. 579, 292 N.W.2d 880 (1980); *Etameny v. Atlantic Richfield Co.*, 164 Cal. Rptr. 839 (Cal. Sup. Ct. 1980); *Pierce v. Ortho Pharmaceutical Corp.*, 84 N.J. 58, 417 A.2d 291 (1980). But, says St. Antoine, "despite these salutary developments . . . the blunt reality is that even in the most enlightened American jurisdictions, unorganized private employers need make no positive showing of cause before ridding themselves of an unwanted employee." *Id.* at 48.

instances, including the entertainment/broadcast field. Often, in public image fields, management will retain the right to release personnel simply because, in management's judgment, the individual is not sufficiently appealing to its clientele. As an alternative to just cause in such situations, the parties may negotiate a provision that at once establishes a severance pay while at the same time making it clear that the discharge need not be based on traditional concepts of just cause.

A standard just cause clause, on the other hand, might read as follows:

> Management agrees that actions taken to discipline or discharge an employee shall be based upon just cause.

Some parties relegate the required just cause to a remedy provision in which it is provided that:

> In cases where an employee has been found to have been discharged or disciplined without just cause, he or she shall be reinstated and made whole for losses suffered.

Even without a collective bargaining agreement, one would intuitively grant management the right to suspend from work and to impose other sanctions in the interest of promoting efficient and desirable behavior. The collectively bargained agreement normally implies the just cause requirement, thereby narrowing managerial prerogatives in the sense that the punishment must be reasonably related to the crime. In reality, it is probably access to the grievance procedure itself, rather than any specified just cause clause that is responsible for this requirement of industrial justice. Just as the managerial right to discipline is assumed, one must also intuitively assume that such right carries with it the responsibility to discipline reasonably.

Discharge of an employee is imposed at the point the misconduct itself is so severe as to be immediately intolerable or, alternatively, at the point the employee's record of offenses is sufficiently extensive that one may reasonably consider corrective measures to have failed. At this point, even though the particular conduct may be relatively less offensive than a so-called "cardinal" matter, the employer will be found to have justified the discharge action.

It is rare that parties will become embroiled in any significant dispute on the existence or nonexistence of just cause under the labor agreement. It is clearly the burden of the party suggesting other than a just cause standard to show its existence. The definition and application of just cause, however, is another matter. It is here that the industrial arena formulates its own set of rules.

The theft case provides a striking example. An employee accused of stealing tools from the plant may face criminal charges as well as the discharge. In court, the prosecutor's burden will be to prove guilt beyond a reasonable doubt. In arbitration, however, the burden on management may differ. Some arbitrators require the "beyond doubt" standard of management in cases where criminal conduct, thus criminal liability, is at issue, on the grounds that termination is the "capital punishment" of labor relations. However, it is generally accepted that in the employment context the employer's obligation is less imposing. Arbitrators have held that the employer must prove the offense with "clear and competent," "persuasive," or, at times, "the preponderance" of the evidence. Reasonable arguments can be made for any one of these approaches. From the union's standpoint, it may be argued that, even assuming one disregards the criminal nature of the events, an employee's present and future livelihood is at stake. Once terminated for theft, that action will haunt and perhaps foreclose any future employment opportunities. Before sustaining the employer's actions in severing the employment, the arbitrator should be absolutely certain that the facts support a finding of guilt. On the other hand, the employer might well argue that a breach of applicable rules and regulations is at stake. At the heart of the matter is, after all, a contractual employment relationship, rather than risk of incarceration, as in criminal proceedings; the proof therefore should be no greater than that existing in the case of any other civil contract matter. As such, whether the penalty is termination or a lesser punishment, it is argued that the arbitrator need only be persuaded by a reasonable preponderance of the evidence.

The same set of hypothetical circumstances reveals another potential difference between just cause in the legal, as opposed to the industrial, relationship. Generally, the industrial concept of discipline draws no distinction between petty and grand larceny. Theft of a hammer and screwdriver from a hardware store might well be considered a misdemeanor and draw a relatively light penalty from a criminal court. But in the shop, theft of such hand tools or other minor items has traditionally and consistently been regarded as proper grounds for discharge, without regard to the value of the items taken or the seniority of the employee. In certain instances, parties have negotiated various understandings as exceptions to the general rule. A major automaker and its union have agreed upon a local rule at one plant providing that a theft of items with less than $25 value by an employee with more than 20 years of service will not necessarily result in automatic discharge. Significantly, however, this is an exception to the general rule, applied on a national basis, that theft of any item of any value will result in an employee's discharge regardless of seniority.

We have seen, then, that differences exist between the public arena, governed by statute and common law, and the private world of the contractual employment relationship. In this latter sphere, parties establish their own categories and hierarchies of conduct. Significant variations exist. It is nevertheless helpful to examine some of these general distinctions.

One may conceive of disciplinary events in general as comprising three categories. The first—those acts that are immediately and substantially destructive of the employment relationship—is often referred to as the "cardinal" violations. Commission of these acts will be grounds for immediate discharge. Usually, but not always, these violations are of a nature that anyone would consider seriously offensive. For the most part, they are what the law refers to as the *malum in se* category of offenses—"evil in themselves"—such as theft or sabotaging equipment. There can be no serious argument over the gravity of such matters, almost without regard to the context. These are to be distinguished from the *malum prohibitum* class—wrong solely because of proscriptive rules. These will be examined later. Smoking in the work place is not intuitively offensive; even smoking in a nonsmoking area might not be considered grounds for summary discharge, absent further information. But if the nonsmoking area is in a dynamite factory, the "cardinal nature" of the violation becomes immediately apparent.

A third category, referred to as "other offenses," includes events which, as will be noted, do not readily fit into the disciplinary context. Excessive absenteeism for bona fide reasons is one example of this group.

Specific Penalties

Employers and unions may seek to codify disciplinary practice by means of contract provisions establishing specific penalties for specific infractions. The advantage of so doing is that the parties—and the employees—obtain a clear understanding of what penalty may be expected in a given situation. There is presumably less opportunity for disparate treatment. The disadvantage is that the employer's lack of flexibility may well result in the necessary imposition of discipline, where, in a particular case, less severe punishment or none at all might have been appropriate.

Additionally, it is rare that such systems will eliminate all arguments. Questions may still arise as to how a particular incident should be categorized. For example, the agreement between certain trucking companies and their employees provides as follows:

Penalties:

Failure to turn in cash bank at end of day

> First offense—warning.
> Second offense—3-day suspension.
> Third offense—discharge.

Dishonesty

> First offense—discharge.

Consider this contract in the context of the following problem.

Big Mike had been employed at the Freeway Transport Company for five years. He was a city driver who made a number of deliveries each day, picking up customer payments at each stop. One day, as Mike left work, his supervisor noticed that the receipts Mike had turned in were $25 short. He asked Mike where the money was. In response, Mike pulled out a roll of cash from his pocket, peeled off $25, and left it at the desk. He apologized, stating he had just cashed his own paycheck and had inadvertently commingled the monies during the day.

The labor agreement provides that failure to turn in funds after a day's run shall be grounds for progressive discipline, including a warning for a first offense. "Dishonesty," on the other hand, is a so-called "cardinal offense" under the labor agreement for which immediate discharge is proper. In this case, Mike was discharged.

Question and Comment

(1) *How should the arbitrator rule?*

The very existence of the lesser penalty ("failure to turn in receipts at the end of the day") is strong evidence that the parties intended to construct a distinction between willful and accidental withholding of funds. In this case, all the evidence and testimony convinced the arbitrator that the withholding was intentional. He sustained the discharge. It goes without saying, however, that essentially similar facts might lead to another conclusion. Thus, under this agreement, given two employees who performed precisely the same act, one might receive a written warning while the other would be discharged. The arbitrator's assessment of the credibility of the grievant's assertions of his intent might be the pivotal factor.

The Cardinal Offenses

Theft is the most universally recognized ground for summary discharge. The overwhelming weight of arbitral authority establishes the general premise that the ultimate penalty will be imposed for theft without regard to the value of the item taken or the length of the employee's service. In the retail food business, for example, discharges have been upheld for taking a can of soda pop, a bar of soap, or a dishrag. Several comments are in order, however. Often, these become the cases that try one's soul. One arbitrator has stated: There are two types of heartbreaking cases. The first is where one reinstates a truly bad employee; the other is where one sustains the discharge of a basically good person. Theft cases can often involve the latter category. And, because arbitrators are human, there is the unavoidable desire to find a way to avoid the ultimate penalty in such cases. Often, there is no question as to the required response in the case of proven theft. But the arbitrators will, in such events, look closely at elements such as whether the particular rule was applied consistently and evenly.

—— **Case** ——

K. Cafritz works in a cookie factory. Posted prominently in the factory are signs stating

Employees may eat as much food (cookies, nuts, raisins, etc.) as they desire during their shift.

However, no amount of any food substance may be removed from this plant at any time.

A violation of this rule will result in immediate discharge.

At her desk, Cafritz maintains a small tin of raisins, which she nibbles on during the day. One day, she works slightly past the end of her shift. Then, hurrying to catch her ride, she closes the tin, which contains a small handful of raisins, places the tin under her arm, and runs for the exit. The guard stops her and asks her to open the tin, which she does. He informs her she cannot remove the raisins from the plant, whereupon she leaves them at the guard shack and goes home.

She is fired the next day. The union grieves and the matter finds its way to arbitration.

Questions and Comments

(1) *Notwithstanding the general rule in theft situations, is the company's rule so unreasonable that an arbitrator should*

overturn it, thus saving grievant's job? Assuming the rule is reasonable, was it applied in a reasonable fashion in this case?

This is a case where the general rule, in industry, of ignoring distinctions between petty and major theft is disturbing. There is a strong tendency simply to conclude that the punishment in this case did not fit the crime. Such a rule may well provide incentive for an arbitrator to search hard for a way to avoid the harsh impact in this case. But compelling arguments can be made in defense of the rule. While it may be that no single incident of food removal would result in a substantial loss to the employer, the cumulative effect could be devastating. In effect, it would grant every employee the right to steal a product once. Such is the position of employers in the retail food business, for example. Arbitrators generally agree that theft of any item from a supermarket will result in an employee's discharge. The items themselves are reasonably inexpensive, but that is all the employer sells and the cumulative effect is significant.

In addition, the rule in this case was widely known and unequivocal. The absolute standard required of employees was an important, specific, and well-known condition of the job, and it is not unreasonable to expect strict compliance.

One might argue that the rule is unreasonable in its failure to distinguish between theft or an intentional taking as opposed to an accidental taking, as was apparently the case here. This is a plausible argument. Was there intent to steal? The difficulty comes in the proof. Cafritz might argue she would hardly have risked long seniority and gainful employment for a few raisins, and that the taking must, by definition, be viewed as accidental. The primary difficulty with this argument is that it is simply too easy to raise. Similarly, it is enormously difficult for the employer to prove intent in this case, given the nature of the items. On such grounds, assuming the underlying propriety of the prohibition, an absolute rule such as the one in this instance is more practicable. In the actual case, the company demonstrated that the rule had been applied and had survived challenge in the past.

(2) *An employee who secreted a cookie in his shirt was discharged and the matter was appealed to arbitration. How-*

ever, the union produced a witness who testified, unrebutted, that as he left the plant one day eating a cookie, the guard detained him and told him to finish the cookie before he left. He did, and there was no further action taken. Would this affect your consideration of the case?

Evidence that the rule has been strictly applied in the past might be crucial in a case such as this. Indeed, contrary evidence indicating condonation may provide an insurmountable problem for the employer. In the case at hand, the arbitrator concluded that if the strict rule were to be sustainable, it must be just as strictly enforced. Evidence that a guard had allowed another employee to avoid its application, and therefore to avoid discharge would probably lead the arbitrator to sustain the grievance.

Another offense normally regarded as cardinal is an employee fighting with a supervisor. In many labor-management relationships, fighting is considered grounds for immediate discharge, but in those cases where a distinction is made, the prohibition with respect to physical violence on supervisors is normally absolute. The basis for this is obvious. The labor relationship is challenged in the extreme when supervisory authority is ignored and the supervisor is intimidated.

In those cases where discharges have been set aside, arbitrators have focused on questions such as supervisory harassment or on the conclusion that the confrontation was, in essence, a joint undertaking. Even then, many of these opinions reflect the fact that the employee's participation was "brief and not reflective of any type of premeditation." Occasionally, a fact question will arise with respect to whether the assault took place on company property and/or during working hours. In the event the confrontation takes place, for example, in a local bar rather than at the plant, it is reasonable to inquire as to the extent to which the event impacts upon the employment relationship. On the one hand, the fact that one of the combatants is a supervisor does not necessarily mean the employer has any interest in an off-duty confrontation. On the other hand, an assault that is in fact work related and intended to intimidate a supervisor is clearly destructive to the day-to-day functioning of the plant and may not be sanctioned merely because it occurred outside the gates. Obviously, these are often extremely difficult fact questions and pose difficult problems of proof for the advocates and the arbitrators.

—— **Case** ——

Charlie Roote ran a sorting machine at the local Widget factory. Late one Friday afternoon, after work, he stopped at his favorite bar and began drinking. After several hours, he was drunk and, as was his nature, in a bad temper. He noticed his supervisor sitting at the other end of the bar and began to make disparaging, loud remarks. Eventually, Roote went over to the supervisor and began a fight. The fight was broken up by local patrons, and both men left. On Monday, Roote was discharged for attacking a supervisor.

At arbitration, the union announced that, while it surely did not condone Roote's actions, they had nothing to do with the work place. Admittedly, Roote had picked on a man he knew, but there was no indication that his antagonism was somehow related to work matters or that it would in any way continue.

The company contended that the serious assault could not help but intimidate the supervisor and thus unavoidably impact the employment relationship.

Questions and Comments

(1) *If you were the arbitrator, how would you rule?*

This is a difficult judgment for the arbitrator to make. The arguments are clear and are properly raised by the parties' positions stated above. Merely because the incident was after hours and off company premises does not mean there will not be an impact on the employment relationship. At the same time, particularly in a large plant, one must recognize that there will be instances of conflict between and among people, and that the employer's interest in "maintaining the employment relationship" may simply not extend to all such disputes.

(2) *Would the situation be different if the grievant had turned to the foreman during working hours and said, menacingly, "I know where you live"?*

Serious threats to supervisors in the work place have traditionally been regarded as serious misconduct. It is more likely that an arbitrator would sustain a discharge in such a case. Admittedly, it is difficult to compare the off-duty fighting with a mere verbal threat and conclude that the threat may be the more serious matter. It is probable, however, that arbitrators are impressed by the inability of the grievant, in the latter situation, to keep antagonisms off the plant floor. In the former situation, the question is whether the discord would be inevitably carried to the work place. In the latter case, doubts as to such carry-over are essentially removed. Some further comment with respect to the threat situation is in order. Threats come in various forms. In each case, the nature of the threat must be carefully evaluated. On the one hand, words that are antagonistic on paper may, in the context of their utterance, be less cause for concern. On the other hand, a comment that is inoffensive in the abstract ("I know where you live") may be considered highly threatening, depending on the circumstances. Often, it is important to consider the impact of the utterance on the one who hears it—perception of the recipient may be of controlling importance. If a remark may reasonably have been taken seriously, it is scarcely relevant that the person who utters it later claims it to be a joke.

Another offense often deemed cardinal in nature is falsification of employment information. Whether a particular misstatement should lead to discharge depends on a variety of factors, including the materiality of the misstatement and the length of time that passed prior to its discovery. In some cases, the substantial nature of the falsification will require the conclusion that, without regard to how long the employee occupied the position, discharge was proper. For example, a bank clerk who previously omitted reference to a long-term prison sentence for embezzlement might be vulnerable for a virtually indefinite period of time. However, as Ford Motor Company UAW Umpire Harry Shulman observed, there is an obligation on the employer to act promptly. Shulman noted that falsification of a material fact that was intended to, and had, the effect of inducing the company to grant employment that would otherwise have been denied, is proper grounds for discharge. However, he said:

> "But a rule that the employee guilty of such falsification is subject to discharge for a reasonable period after the employer first learns of the falsification, whenever that may be, would also be unduly harsh and capricious. It, too, would provide for no definite time limit. In addition, it would put a premium on the employer's failure to ascertain the truth. And the fate of employees similarly situated would depend entirely upon the pure chance of when the employer happened to learn of the falsification."[2]

In that case, the umpire imposed a one-year time limitation on the life of such cause of action by the employer.

—— Case ——

Lisa applied for work as a flight attendant with an airlines in February 1977. Her employment application noted that from 1970 to 1974 she was employed by the A & B Bakeries. In fact, however, she had worked for another airline company during that time and had been discharged for misconduct.

In July 1980, Lisa volunteered the truth to a company supervisor. She was fired.

At the arbitration, the union argued that Lisa's misconduct had to be considered in light of a reasonably long and wholly satisfactory employment record. Additionally, it noted that the grievant herself approached the company to divulge the falsification.

The company directed the arbitrator's attention to a clear-cut rule against falsifying company records.

---

[2]Opinion A-184 (May 4, 1945), at 341.

154 Labor Agreement in Negotiation and Arbitration

This, it claimed, was falsification of such a material nature that discharge was appropriate.

Question and Comment

(1) *How would the arbitrator decide?*

One may assume that the company regulations concerning falsification are clear and that grievant was well advised as to the risk and the penalties. The case is reasonably difficult, since the job tenure of about three and one-half years is neither notably short nor significantly long. Arbitration precedent in this area tends to be diverse. Some arbitrators establish per se time limits. Others scrutinize the entire scope of the circumstances, given the nature of the falsification, the length of the employee's tenure, and the overall state of his or her work record to determine whether there is cause for mitigation. Arbitrators have held, in a case such as this, that mitigation was appropriate, considering that grievant took steps to disclose her past. Note that this case is not one where present misconduct led to the discovery of a past deceit. The fundamental assumption in such cases is that the offense is one for which discharge is appropriate. The overall analysis proceeds with an inquiry as to whether circumstances exist that warrant mitigation.

Lesser Offenses and Progressive Discipline

Beyond the cardinal offenses, there is a second class of misconduct that may lead to summary discharge and is usually readily identifiable as offensive in and of itself. However, the precepts of progressive discipline, whether explicitly set forth in the labor agreement or not, are more readily applied in this area. As a result, commission of these offenses may yield a discharge situation and may also generate discipline short of discharge in certain relationships.

The nature and extent of the discipline will depend in some cases upon specific agreement of the parties and is likely to take into consideration such items as mitigating circumstances, employee length of service, practice of the parties, arbitration precedent, and other factors.

Employee insubordination is one example of such misconduct. On the one hand, there can hardly be a more severe challenge to the industrial relationship than the refusal of an employee to obey a supervisory order. Yet, arbitrators have routinely considered the nature of the order, the relationship between the particular supervisor and employee, evidence of harassment, disparate treatment of similarly situated employees, length of service, and other items in evaluating the extent of the penalty.

—— **Case** ——

Consider the following varieties of facts:

(1) Joe Jones is an equipment service employee for an airline. One day, his supervisor said, "Joe, would you please work on the east ramp for the rest of the morning? I've had some unexpected absentee problems." Joe refuses and walks away.

(2) Same situation, but the supervisor says, "Joe, I'm trying to figure out how to cover absenteeism at the east ramp. Would you have any objection to working there this morning?" Joe says, "Yes, I will not work there."

(3) Assume Joe is called to the supervisor's office after either of the above encounters. In the office, the supervisor says, "Sit down, Joe, I want to talk to you about the assignment I gave." Joe replies, "Thanks, but I'll stand." "When I conduct a disciplinary interview, Joe," says the supervisor, "I expect the employee to be seated. I'm giving you a direct order to sit down." Joe refuses.

Question and Comment

(1) *Consider the above situations. Is the first case to be distinguished from the second? Is the supervisor justified in charging insubordination in the third case?*

As indicated earlier, there is no real question that the refusal of a direct supervisory order may properly be considered insubordination. But there must be a direct order. It is possible that objective observers will distinguish between the first and second cases, finding there was a direct order in the first situation but none in the second. There is no magic formula for determining what constitutes a direct order. Note that the order in the first case came in the form of a reasonably polite question. Nevertheless, one may not reasonably conclude that the employee had room, under those circumstances, to refuse the request.

In Case 2, on the other hand, the supervisor appears to have been soliciting the employee's feelings about the task rather than actually assigning it. Under these circumstances, one might hold that a direct order was not issued.

The third case raises the issue of the potential abuse of supervisory discretion. Penalties for insubordination are potentially harsh. At the same time, it is reasonable to require that the orders issued be directly related to the work or production process. To be sure, an employee must be cooperative in the context of labor relations functions as well as pure production. But in the instance cited above, there was no real challenge to supervisory authority by the employee's standing rather than sitting during the interview. Arbitrators have overturned discipline based on such incidents, finding that the insubordination charge was overly severe.

The "Other" Cases

The third category of offenses is reserved for a variety of employee conduct which, while either immediately or eventually intolerable, nevertheless may not be categorized as necessarily reflecting "fault" on the part of the employee. Poor workmanship, for example, raises certain problems in the purely disciplinary context. In response, employers have often imposed progressive discipline leading to termination or, at times, demotion.

—— Case ——

George T. runs a large production saw. He has been with the Ajax Company for 30 years and has always performed the same job. In recent months, however, management has noticed what it believes to be a drop in the quality of George's work. Accordingly, after a number of discussions and written warnings, management demotes George to a lower paying job as a sawyer-helper. Initially, management refuses to arbitrate the matter, contending that demotions are purely within its managerial prerogatives. It cites the portion of the labor agreement that states:

> Management shall retain all discretionary authority to hire, fire, promote, demote, and to manage the business in the best exercise of its judgment. It is agreed, however, that discipline and discharge shall be for just cause only.

The union argues that, in effect, management has merely imposed a significant and enormously harsh disciplinary penalty by lowering George's wage rate for the remainder of his working career. Short of firing the employee, says the union, management could hardly have imposed more severe discipline.

Question and Comment

(1) *How should the arbitrator respond?*

These are often troublesome cases from both a conceptual and a factual standpoint. The contract language in question rather clearly removes the demotion action from the area of just cause, inasmuch as it is grouped among those employer actions designated as within management's sole discretion. Moreover, the just cause standard is rather clearly applied simply to discipline and discharge actions. (Note, however, that the authority to "fire" as well as "hire," while listed as a management right, would certainly be held to a just cause standard.)

There is a wide diversity of arbitral opinion in this area. Many neutrals simply treat demotions as necessarily disciplinary and conclude that, notwithstanding contractual suggestions to the contrary, as in the above example, management must prove just cause. The best approach would appear to treat demotions as discipline when, in fact, they are. Such treatment is appropriate, for even assuming there are some demotions that are simply an exercise of management's rights to properly place an employee in the appropriate job, there are others that reflect punishment for misconduct. How does one distinguish? No rule will ease the notably difficult fact-finding task. However, it may be said that when the concern is with a lapse, rather than a lack, in ability, a disciplinary response is in order. The difficulty with the case set forth above, from a fact-finding standpoint, is in determining whether the employee was suffering a spell of laziness or sloppiness (a "lapse" in otherwise acceptable work) or whether, instead, he was becoming increasingly unable to perform the job. In this case, length of service and age might be used to justify either position. That is why the fact-finding portion of this type of dispute is so difficult.

Absenteeism because of bona fide illness, to be discussed in greater detail below, is another case where discipline is often imposed (and sustained by arbitrators) yet where it may not accurately be said the employee is at "fault." These cases, and others such as alcohol and drug addiction, may not be readily classified among the general run-of-the-mill disciplinary events.

Areas raising significant and continuous problems in arbitration are those in which conduct occurs that urgently requires modification or discontinuation, but where application of punitive disciplinary measures are somehow incongruous. For example, employees who are chronically ill and who, as a result, encounter consistently more severe absentee problems raise just such troublesome issues. On the one hand, it is abundantly clear that the situation must change. On the other hand, suspending a person or imposing discipline of one type or another will hardly cure a disability or illness. The alternatives—terminating individuals without some sort of warning action or maintaining them on the employment rolls indefinitely—are acceptable to neither the company nor the union.

Absenteeism and Arbitration[3]

Absenteeism is one of the most significant problems in industrial labor relations today. The magnitude of the problem is in large part reflected by the widespread misunderstanding concerning various contract provisions and disciplinary procedures involved with absenteeism, particularly that caused by illness. The purpose of this discussion is to review some of these areas and to provide some insight.

Progressive Discipline

In response to the employee who is careless about attendance—who is often tardy or absent without reasonable cause—progressive discipline makes sense. Ideally, the recognition that his or her job is increasingly in jeopardy will motivate the individual to report in a more timely and consistent manner.

If the individual is truly ill, discipline is obviously futile, at least in terms of curing the illness and correcting the problem. This does not mean, however, that progressive discipline or, alternatively, clear notification to an employee that his job tenure is at stake, will not be required as a precondition to termination.

—— Case ——

Susan Lowe was a long-tenured and valued employee in the front office of the Westmount School District. For 25 years, she had performed a wide range of important clerical functions and became one of those precious employees who, virtually single-handedly, "run the business." However, through a series of unfortunate medical problems, Ms. Lowe was forced to take a series of extended leaves. Over a period of one year, she missed almost 40 percent of her working days. Management met with Ms. Lowe and told her her attendance would have to improve or it would be

[3]Certain portions of the following materials first appeared in the Prentice-Hall Industrial Relations Guide Service in 1980. Permission to reprint is hereby acknowledged with the authors' thanks. See ¶42, 165.

necessary for them to dismiss her. Unfortunately, her condition improved only slightly and, during the following two months, she missed an additional 10 working days. Accordingly, management terminated her.

At arbitration, the union argues that, so long as the grievant's illness is bona fide, management may not remove her from the work rolls. It recognized Ms. Lowe's critical position but argues that management must, if necessary, transfer her to a less demanding job prior to terminating her. It notes that such accommodations have been made in the past for other employees.

Management contends that it simply cannot tolerate the level of absenteeism this employee has sustained. At some point, it says, it has the right to make the decision to terminate.

Question and Comment

(1) *How should the arbitrator decide?*

Excessive absenteeism resulting from unavoidable health problems is as serious a threat to the employment relationship as is excessive absenteeism due to malingering. While this is obvious, the conclusion that either type of absenteeism may eventually constitute grounds for termintion is often ignored or misunderstood. The employment relationship is a two-way street. As a general rule, the employer is obligated, subject to the varying needs of the business, to provide employment on a continuing basis. But the employee assumes obligations as well. He or she must report for work in a reasonably timely and consistent fashion to uphold that end of the bargain. If the employee is unable or unwilling to do so, the employer is justified in terminating the relationship because of the grievant's unwillingness or inability to provide the contracted-for services. This is true even though there is no real question as to the bona fide nature of the employee's disability; the absenteeism and the impact on the employer are nonetheless severe.

Surely, this does not resolve the numerous questions that

will exist as to when and under what circumstances absentee-ism is to be considered excessive; no one may reasonably ex-pect that a worker will never be ill. But the concept that an employee is entitled to keep the job, as long as absences are based upon bona fide illness or disability (absent agreement by the parties to this effect) is a misconception.

Sick Days

Collective bargaining agreements often incorporate stipu-lated numbers of days an employee earns during a given period of time to be used for illness. It would scarcely seem necessary to emphasize that such days are to be utilized only in cases of illness. Often, however, they are looked upon by employees in the nature of vacation days and thus abused. Employers are well within their rights in responding to this with disciplinary action that can range anywhere from unexcused absence to absent-without-leave charges, which, in the latter case, may well carry more serious, and more immediate, discipline. These are traditional and well-accepted notions.

Clearly, sick days are a bank of sorts upon which an em-ployee may draw to avoid loss of pay during illness. But do they also act to guarantee continuity of employment so long as their numbers are not exceeded? The answer to this is far less clear.

Take, for example, the individual who accumulates one day per month of sick leave. If, after eight months' service, that employee were sick for eight consecutive days, there is little question (assuming, of course, a bona fide illness) that he or she would be exercising a contractual right to be off work, to be paid to the extent provided by contract, and to return to work later without penalty. In a recent case, the parties had provided for 12 days of annual sick leave. An employee was formally warned for using eight days in a 10-month period since this was above the average usage. The action followed company policy on excessive absenteeism. However, an arbitrator found that this policy violated the collective bargaining agreement; the employer could not, on the one hand, promise the availabil-ity of the days and then discipline the worker for using them.

But this raises the difficult issue and the specific question of whether the sick days necessarily amount to a guarantee of continued employment. Assume, for example, that the collective bargaining agreement established 12 days per year sick leave, with full accumulation of unused days from year to year. Assume further that a three-year employee had had a poor attendance record, with absences incurred for a variety of reasons. During the most recent year, the employee was off for one month with an industrial injury and six days of unexcused absences. Management suspended the employee on a number of occasions with the warning that continued excessive absenteeism would lead to discharge. Yet, shortly thereafter, the employee contracted a severe case of pneumonia. Assume the employee had some 20 days of sick leave left. Was it incumbent upon management to retain the employee but only for the duration of his sick leave? Could it terminate the employee at all, inasmuch as the absence was illness-related?

These are troublesome issues. On the one hand, if one concludes that management may not discharge so long as the absence is illness-related and so long as there are sick leave days remaining in the bank, then one must also conclude that excessive absenteeism is to be tolerated in at least this one instance of actual illness. There is nothing inherently improper or illogical about such a conclusion. But the contrary argument is also compelling; absent express language by the parties on the subject, you might readily conclude that while the employer is obliged to pay for the sick leave days earned, this does not necessarily guarantee a return to employment. Such a position would comply with contractual demands in terms of satisfying the employee's earned benefits, while at the same time remaining consistent with the premise that the employment bargain is a two-way street.

These are not mere hypothetical games. An industry or plant where the work force is composed of older, senior people may well encounter the serious dilemma of a long-term dedicated employee increasingly afflicted with chronic health problems and result in intolerable attendance records. Competing concerns of employer loyalty versus requisite productivity raise serious and difficult questions. That arbitrators have taken a variety of positions on this subject should be no surprise, given the varied theoretical considerations. The lesson to be learned is that the parties must establish, with some specificity, by which rules they intend to be bound.

Sick Slips

Often employees will be required (usually because of a poor attendance record) to produce documentation when illness occurs in the future. In many cases, this will take the form of some verification by a physician that the employee was, indeed, under the doctor's care for the period in question. A number of problems arise in this area. The employee who is disciplined or discharged for failure to produce a doctor's slip often responds with the plea that he or she simply did not think it necessary to secure the slip when it was obviously a garden variety flu bug or heavy cold for which a doctor's services would not normally be sought. When the need for such documentation is announced in advance, this defense will be unavailing. Normally, the employee's past performance will have made this requirement necessary, and the claim that circumstances made it unreasonable to see a doctor will generally be of little value.

Difficult cases often arise wherein, while a doctor's slip per se will not be required, some evidence supporting the claim for illness might reasonably be expected. An employee who is off weekends, for example, and who has consistent absences on Mondays and Fridays, will at some point be required to do more than merely claim illness. If management has previously warned the employee about continued absenteeism under such circumstances, it is not unreasonable to require him or her to take particular care to support the claim of yet another recurring illness. The form of such evidence may vary, but, as a general matter, in cases where abuse is a realistic prospect, the burden will fall on the employee to justify an absence. This will be so even without the specific preannounced requirement of a medical slip.

In this regard, a comment concerning doctors' slips is in order. On the one hand, one must recognize that, in terms of a physician-patient relationship, the doctor's interest is on the side of the patient. If the patient indicates discomfort and is upset, it is to be expected that a doctor will advise staying away from work and, upon request, provide evidence of such orders. On the other hand, in certain locations, the availability of so-called "$5 slips"—excuses written upon demand by a physician or the physician's office staff—is well known. If it can be shown that the slip was executed in a perfunctory manner, perhaps with no actual examination by the physician, the employee may be asked to provide more concrete evidence of his treatment—perhaps to the extent of testimony by the physician.

The content of such medical certificates is often subject to challenge as to completeness. For a medical certificate to be given the greatest weight, it should contain the following:

(1) a diagnosis of the ailment,
(2) the clinical symptoms that constitute the basis of that diagnosis,
(3) the ideology of the ailment,
(4) the basis for finding that ideology,
(5) the prognosis, and
(6) any impact that the foregoing might have on the employee's work.

A variation on this theme sometimes occurs when an employee is, for one reason or another, unable to produce the doctor's excuse originally, but later (perhaps in the grievance procedure or at arbitration) submits the slip. At that time, the employee might claim the slip was originally misplaced or that, while he or she originally forgot to obtain it during the visit, it was secured at a later time. This may raise doubts as to the veracity of the documentation. But assuming the employee has received medical treatment and failed to submit a doctor's slip, what should the employer do? The employer is not to be faulted for disciplining the employee based on what it knew at the time of the incident, particularly if the employee had been on express notice to provide such proof. At the same time (and, again assuming the veracity of the slip), the underlying goal of securing a doctor's examination and providing proof of it has been satisfied.

In such cases, arbitrators have often reinstated employees on the basis of their having successfully supported the claim of illness. However, because the employee, through failure to produce the required documentation at an earlier stage, had inspired the continuing controversy, arbitrators have apportioned the burden of the ensuing dispute by reinstating without back pay.

–––––– **Case** ––––––

    Selma had used up five of her six days of annual sick leave by the time she called in on April 4 and said she was suffering stomach cramps and was unable to work. Her supervisor challenged her claim and asked her to bring in a physician's note covering the absence on her return to work. This she failed to do and was denied the day's pay, giving rise to the instant grievance and arbitration.

Questions and Comments

(1) *If you were the arbitrator, how would you rule?*

    There is no question of the employer's right to assume that employees taking sick leave have a bona fide reason to do so. In determining whether the claims of sick leave are legitimate, the employer may properly request the provision of a physician's certificate as to legitimacy of the absence. Such a request for medical certification may be viewed as harsh if required in all cases of absence, but would probably be held acceptable in situations where the employer had reasonable cause for suspicion. For example, if all prior sick days immediately preceded or followed a holiday, or if it had evidence that the grievant had been seen shopping on prior sick days, the employer would be considered to have reasonable grounds for the request. The fact that it was asked of Selma and not of other employees on their sixth absence might be viewed as discriminatory by some arbitrators but would probably be viewed by most as a legitimate exercise of the employer's policing authority in cases where there were reasonable grounds for suspecting the honesty of the employee's claim.

(2) *What if the employee brought in a doctor's certificate that said merely, "Selma was ill on April 4, complaining of stomach cramps"? Would the employer be justified in rejecting such a note? What if the note were never produced until the arbitration hearing, the employer disciplined the employee*

> *for not bringing in a doctor's certificate, and the employee grieved the discipline bringing in the doctor's certificate at the arbitration hearing?*

The acceptability of the physician's certificate would depend on what the employer requested either in its administrative rules or explicitly of the grievant. Many employers request certificates stating that the employee was unable to work on the day in question, while others require evidence of a doctor's visit that day. The employer is within its rights in rejecting a physician's statement that it believes does not meet its standards or, even if properly executed, it believes was fraudulently secured but it does so at its own risk. The arbitrator is probably more concerned with establishing the legitimacy of the absence than conformity to the employer's rules. Thus if the certificate were rejected by the company because it did not state that Selma was unable to work, or that the physician examined her, or, indeed, even that Selma in fact had stomach cramps, it would run the risk of having the arbitrator sustain the grievance if the evidence or the doctor's testimony persuaded him or her that Selma was, indeed, incapable of working that day.

As suggested above, if the employee had been disciplined for not bringing in a doctor's certificate and then finally brought in the doctor's certificate at the arbitration hearing, most arbitrators would sustain the employee's actions as being appropriate based on the evidence it then had in hand. The arbitrator might reinstate the grievant without back pay if the certificate were deemed credible, but the deprivation of back pay would be imposed because of the employee's duty to take all reasonable steps to avoid the resulting dispute.

(3) *Would the employer be justified in imposing discipline for what it believed to be an excessive amount of absenteeism if the grievant were sick for all six of the contractual sick days while all other employees took no more than four such days per year?*

Although the employer has the right to protect against abuse of the sick leave entitlement, the fact that it agreed to six days of available sick leave per year demonstrates that at least at the time of signing the contract, it believed employees should be permitted to take off six days for illness per year. The subsequent evidence—that all other employees took no more than four days of such leave per year—does not detract from the grievant's entitlement to six days for legitimate illness. Certainly the employer could discipline for fraudulent use of sick days but if an employee were actually sick for all six days, most arbitrators would find that he or she was immune from discipline therefor.

(4) *As an arbitrator, would you deny a claim for sick pay on a day when the supervisor went to the grievant's residence and found him gone?*

Most arbitrators would hold that the employer has the authority to monitor claims of sick pay in cases where it has reasonable grounds for suspecting fraudulent use of such leave. But while they would probably admit testimony as to the results of the visits, it would not be conclusive proof of fraudulent use of sick leave. The employee would have the opportunity, and the responsibility, to show that he or she was absent, at the doctor's office or the pharmacy, at a parent's home or elsewhere for legitimate and presumably illness-related reasons, and was indeed ill and unable to work.

Absentee Programs

In an effort to combat the problems of excessive absenteeism, employers have responded in a variety of ways, often in consultation or even negotiation with unions. At times, specific absentee programs are incorporated in the collective bargaining agreements. More often, they are not and simply exist as company policy. But the policies often come under fire in the grievance procedure.

It is inordinately difficult to draft a "trouble-free" absentee policy. Many employers refrain from announcing a particular level of absenteeism to be considered excessive or abusive, preferring instead to handle the issues on a case-by-case basis. Theoretically, this is ideal. The problem, however, is that such a system is vulnerable to charges of disparate or discriminatory treatment. In response to this, other employers have established set standards to be applied on an across-the-board basis. These programs may be attacked as unreasonable and inflexible to the particular aspects of a single employee's situation. Thus, employers are often caught in a "damned if you do, damned if you don't" squeeze.

There is no ready solution to this problem. As a general matter, it must be remembered that even the most responsive and carefully drafted policy will be challenged in a given case on grounds of just cause. And, this is wholly appropriate; there should be room for testing the principles against the particular facts. What follows is a brief listing of some of the more frequent areas where programs themselves are found lacking by arbitrators and, therefore, where discipline or discharge based upon such programs is set aside:

(1) *Lack of identifiable standards.* This, in itself, may not be a problem. The trouble arises when the lack of standards results in disparate treatment; one supervisor may decide that a certain employee's absences should be treated considerably more harshly than a similarly situated worker under another supervisor. In such instances, employers may find it difficult to sustain the more severe penalty.

(2) *Inflexible standards.* Standards that leave no room for mitigation on the basis of good cause are vulnerable to successful challenge.

(3) *"Undisclosed" standards.* If employees are given no guidance as to what level of attendance performance is expected, it may well be contended that strict adherence may not be required.

(4) *Incomprehensible program.* In a number of cases, management's attempts to formulate a program that may be applied to every conceivable variation (Should three absences on Fridays be counted the same as three absences on Wednesdays? Should one absence of seven days be viewed the same as seven absences of one day?) lead to the construction of programs that are virtually incomprehensible to all beyond the drafters. Here, too, the danger is that employees may well be found not to have been put on proper notice as to the expected level of compliance.

By reviewing the above list of pitfalls, one might conclude there is no way to draft a satisfactory program. Hopefully, this is not true. But, like the absences at issue, the programs themselves must be judged on a case-by-case basis. There is no reason to expect that any given program will be wholly immune to challenge in a given case. Yet, if it serves to establish reasonable standards of required attendance, is effectively communicated to the work force, and provides sufficient room to respond to unique circumstances, the policy should serve both the employer and the employee well.

Alcohol and Drug Dependency

Fewer areas are more troublesome in the context of discipline than cases involving alcohol and drug dependency. There is no lack of either literature or overall concern about the massive and widespread industrial problems generated by these afflictions. Yet each case seems to generate new concerns for the parties, and the process is all too often a re-invention of the wheel. There are numerous troublesome aspects. Is the condition to be treated like a disease? What weight is to be given to the existence or nonexistence of a work-related rehabilitation program? What authority does the arbitrator have in fashioning remedies in this area—is it permissible, absent acquiescence by the parties, for the arbitrator to effect a "conditional reinstatement" wherein the employee's return to work is contingent upon successful completion of a rehabilitation program? What of the impact of applicable state or federal statutes with respect to treatment of alcoholics, for example, as handicapped persons?

——— Case ———

Phillip Mitchell and Paul Legion are power plant engineers at a nuclear reactor site. Both are in charge of monitoring the main plant. Their shifts run from midnight to 8:00 a.m. Plant rules, posted conspicuously, provide as follows:

The following shall be cause for immediate discharge:

(1) Theft
(2) Fighting
(3) Sleeping on the job.

One night, Phillip comes to work exhausted. He has never fully adjusted to the midnight shift and, not having slept well during the day, he spent the evening at the movies. Paul has slept well enough during the day, but spent the evening drinking. He is an alcoholic.
Both men fall asleep on the job. Both are fired.

Question and Comment

(1) *If alcoholism is to be considered an illness, should this be seen as mitigation for Paul only? Would your answer be different if both had been drinking, but only Paul was an alcoholic? What if Phillip were taking medicine for a cold that made him drowsy while Paul had simply "tied one on"?*

The obligation to treat alcoholism as a disease does not necessarily require that it be considered as mitigation for all misconduct. In every case, the circumstances, both of the job requirements and the individual's condition, may be relevant.

There are no ready answers applicable across the board. On the one hand, alcoholism may be distinguished from other illnesses by the individual's ability to control, to varying degrees, his or her own behavior. On the other hand, the fundamental problem is normally that of recognition. Accordingly, the employee may well engage in job-related misconduct before being brought to the point of recognition.

In the above examples, it is conceivable that Paul would be held equally accountable for taking cold medicine on the job as would Phillip for getting drunk. Particularly in a position where such a high premium is placed on alertness, it may well be that he should have reported off rather than risk the drowsiness that is often a side effect of some medications.

Increasingly, alcoholism is being viewed as a disease. This is as it should be. Companies and unions are now, more so than before, cooperating in the establishment and administration of counseling and rehabilitation programs. The same approach has not been as widespread in the context of drug and chemical dependency. But even when viewed as a disease, addiction cases are different from say, a chronic illness. They are afflictions that, to varying degrees, may be controlled by behavior modification and dedication to treatment. Unlike other illnesses, progressive discipline may not only be helpful but conceivably essential to correcting the problem. The difficulty comes in determining the extent of the employer's responsibility in these areas. Moreover, one may reasonably distinguish jobs where alcohol offenses are clearly and immediately intolerable—a crane operator or an airline pilot, for example—in contrast to others where the danger to fellow employees or to others might be less imminent.

The problem is in somehow establishing a program that is meaningfully responsive to the problem of the afflicted employee while at the same time protecting the employer's obvious interest in a safe and efficient work force.

Some companies attempt to accommodate this problem by establishing a rehabilitation program along with the requirement that, to be eligible for the program, the employee must come forward voluntarily. Involvement in an alcohol-related offense, on the other hand, before stepping forward, often amounts to summary discharge. The hope is to attract the alcoholic to the rehabilitation program while at the same time impressing him or her with the knowledge that an on-the-job alcohol violation will certainly result in discharge. Other companies may tolerate a first offense but then suspend the individual pending treatment, under the theory that such an "encounter" is necessary to bring the alcoholic to the full realization of the tenuous nature of his or her continued employment. One need not conjecture as to the relative merits of these programs. Suffice it to say, however, that, in the context of a just cause inquiry, arbitrators will often distinguish.

Remedies

One of the most troublesome areas in discipline and discharge cases concerns remedies for violation of the just cause provision. In most cases the creation of the appropriate remedy is left to the discretion of the arbitrator. Some parties attempt to settle certain questions by means of the contract. Such efforts rarely extend to answering many of the common questions that could be set to rest through specific language. On the one hand, no bargained language could cover every fact situation (although a number of contracts set to rest the entire question simply by providing that grievant will be reinstated with full back pay if he or she prevails, regardless of any other circumstances). On the other hand, it is also true that the parties rarely argue the question of remedy before the neutral at the arbitration hearing. This presents numerous problems, which will be examined below. The burden of anticipating these problems and discussing them or, if necessary, taking evidence on the issue, should be jointly shared. The arbitrator must properly inquire as to the appropriate remedies, and the parties must be prepared to examine the various possibilities.

There are a number of recurrent questions following reinstatement of a discharged employee or the setting aside of a disciplinary suspension:

(1) *Does an employee normally continue to accrue seniority during a disciplinary suspension?*

This is an important aspect of the make whole remedy. For example, there are many cases where discharges are set aside, but the employee is returned to work without back pay. The time off is considered to be a disciplinary suspension. But what about seniority? If an employee's seniority normally does not accrue during a suspension period, then it should not accrue in these circumstances. But absent specific practice and guidance on this point, the reinstatement will normally be with seniority, even if back pay is forfeited.

(2) *What provisions are to be made for interim income? Are earnings from other employment to be offset against the back pay? Should the employee be required to show that he or she looked for work in the interim? What about unemployment compensation receipts?*

In *F. W. Woolworth Company*, 90 NLRB 289 (1950), the National Labor Relations Board set forth its rule for computing back pay. It did so according to the following principles:[4]

---

[4] In *NLRB v. Seven-Up Bottling Co.*, 344 U.S. 344 (1953), the Supreme Court approved the formula but suggested it might be modified when a seasonal industry is involved.

"(1) The loss is calculated on the basis of each separate calendar quarter (or portion) from the date of the unlawful discharge to the date of a proper offer of reinstatement.

"(2) Loss is determined by deducting net earnings for each quarter from the amount the employee normally would have earned. 'Net earnings' means earnings minus expenses incurred in seeking and performing alternative employment."

It is interesting to note that the NLRB computed back pay on a quarterly basis for two reasons. First, many employees secure higher paying jobs following the unlawful discharge. In such cases, the greater the delay in offering reinstatement, the greater the reduction of back pay liability if calculated over the entire period; this method was seen as an incentive for the employer to avoid foot-dragging. Second, quarterly computation allows the parties to monitor their accruing rights and obligations on the basis of then-current conditions not subject to later fluctuation. While arbitrators split over the question, the NLRB has refused to deduct unemployment compensation receipts from back-pay liabilities.[5]

(3) *What about interest? Is an employee entitled to interest on sums withheld? If so, at what rate?*

It is rare, indeed, that an arbitrator will award interest on back pay. On the one hand, one might argue that such interest is a natural consequence of the denied salary, is necessary to truly make the employee whole, and should be awarded. Courts routinely grant interest on improperly withheld sums.

But in the labor relations context, it is virtually unheard of for arbitrators to award interest on back-pay awards in grievance arbitration. Why this is the case is not entirely clear. The most immediate answer seems to be that it simply has never been done that way. Employers and unions have traditionally looked to restoration of wages as the ultimate financial remedy to the extent that, should a contrary result be desired, it would be incumbent upon the parties to specify it with express language. This is properly viewed as a rule peculiar to the labor relations context. But in that arena, it is by no means unheard of. The National Labor Relations Act was established in 1935.

---

[5] See *NLRB v. Gullett Gin Co.*, 340 U.S. 361 (1951).

Yet, it was not until 1962, in *Isis Plumbing and Heating Co.*[6] that the NLRB began to add six percent interest to back pay due to employees wrongfully discharged. This practice was upheld in *Philip Carey Mfg. Co. v. NLRB.*[7] At least one commentator has characterized this phenomenon as an aspect of "specific enforcement." That is, looking strictly at the question of what would have happened had the labor contract been properly administered, the individual would have received wages only, without interest. But this explanation seems somehow unsatisfactory. In the final analysis, the only clear reason before the general denial of interest is that this is the way it has always been done, and is therefore fully in accord with the parties' expectation. A qualification is in order. With the burgeoning of public sector bargaining and interest arbitration (arbitration of new contract terms), arbitrators have, on occasion, granted interest on retroactive salary adjustments. While it is not the intent here to explore the philosophy of that particular aspect of arbitration, suffice it to say that the establishment of retroactive pay rates under a new contract differs significantly from a "damage" award in a grievance arbitration case.

(4) *Assuming a back-pay award for "wages lost," does this include overtime wages and, if so, how should the overtime hours one "would have worked" be ascertained?*

The overall intent of the remedial scheme is to put the employee in a position he or she would have been in had the violation not occurred. If it may be shown that the employee had, in fact, worked a pattern of consistent overtime hours, there is no reason why a back-pay order should not include those sums. Admittedly, there may be some uncertainty involved in such calculations, but with due regard for avoiding sheer speculation, uncertainties must, in these instances, be resolved against the breaching party.

(5) *How, practically speaking, should these questions be resolved?*

---

[6]138 NLRB 716 (1962).
[7]331 F.2d 720 (6th Cir.), cert. denied, 379 U.S. 888 (1964).

In practice, the parties spend notably little time in discussing the remedial aspect of an arbitration case. Arbitrators often are loath to solicit their views for fear it will be seen as "tipping" one's hand. Moreover, arbitrators routinely assume these questions will be ironed out by the parties; therefor, the matters are often remanded to the parties for such purposes. This is a reasonable procedure and, in the majority of cases, it presents no practical problems. But there are instances where the parties will be unable to resolve even these remedial matters. It may then be necessary to approach the same or another arbitrator to resolve that dispute.

Some discussion is in order concerning the question of retaining jurisdiction. Absent the parties' express request to do so, arbitrators should not unilaterally assume that they may retain jurisdiction over the question of damages. In a 1981 report to the National Academy of Arbitrators, Chairman of the Legal Affairs Committee, John Kagel, reported that, in California state courts, superior court judges are being urged to vacate awards where arbitrators remand back pay or other aspects of remedy but retain jurisdiction in the event the parties do not resolve the remanded matter. This procedure has apparently passed muster under federal law.[8] But in California, at least one court has overturned such an award on the basis that it was, "incomplete." Evidently, a specific stipulation by the parties that the arbitrator could retain jurisdiction would have cured the fatal defect in that case.

In sum, many parties become adept at resolving these "left overs" internally or by stipulation at the arbitration hearing. In other cases, however, the questions posed above, and others, present a continuing source of dissatisfaction and dispute.

—— Case ——

Chris Giordano was discharged for alleged theft. At the hearing, however, another employee confessed and Giordano was reinstated with instructions by the arbitrator that the grievant be made whole for "all wages and other benefits lost."

---

[8]See *Safeway Stores v. Teamsters Local 70*, 83 Cal. 3d 430, 147 Cal. Rptr. 835, 99 LRRM 2929 (1978). See also 98 LRRM 2795 (1978).

Questions and Comments

(1) *During the period he was off, his medical coverage lapsed. Without income he could not secure replacement coverage. Then, he incurred a $2500 hospital bill. What decision would you as the arbitrator make?*

The question of health insurance is often misunderstood. First, it is true that hospitalization benefits were cut off at the time of discharge. Had the grievant incurred no expense, however, these premium payments would not be reimbursable, for he lost nothing in the interim. In the facts stated above, he paid a $2500 hospital bill. A general duty to mitigate might lead some arbitrators to find he should have covered himself by securing other insurance during the time off. Assuming he was unable to do so without an incoming salary, the company would be liable for such payments.

Note that these are purely contractual payments. It is conceivable that the grievant may have incurred other substantial losses during his time off. He may, for example, have been unable to continue car payments, and thus have suffered a repossession or mortgage foreclosure. The overwhelming majority of arbitration opinions, however, will not recognize this type of loss. The theory is, that in the context of the labor agreement, the parties contemplated only reimbursement for contractual benefits denied.

(2) *Following his discharge, Giordano's co-workers who accepted overtime assignments averaged 15 hours per week. During the period of his employment, grievant had declined all weekend overtime assignments and many weekday opportunities. He had never averaged more than 10 hours per week overtime. Moreover, in the 30 days preceding his discharge, he had accepted no overtime. As arbitrator, how would you decide?*

The obligation to "make whole" requires that an individual be put in the position that he or she would have been in had the contract breach not occurred. It is relevant, then, to examine the overtime opportunities available during the period of absence. But it is also appropriate to consider whether the grievant could have been expected to have worked these assignments. Reasonable projections may be made, but undue speculation must be avoided. One may conclude from this set of facts that overtime was available if desired, at least to the extent of 15 hours per week. But it is also significant that the grievant had never worked more than 10 overtime hours a week and would probably not have done so during this period. Moreover, one must scrutinize the reason for not having accepted the assignments within 30 days of the discharge. If, for example, he was suffering from a back injury, it may be that he could not have been expected to work. A back-pay award that encompassed overtime under those circumstances would be a windfall inasmuch as it would put the grievant in a better position than he would have been had he been working.

(3) *While off work, Giordano had received unemployment compensation totaling 80 percent of his salary. How would you rule as arbitrator?*

The majority of arbitration awards will provide reimbursement for earnings lost, usually without specific reference to unemployment compensation, leaving that to the parties, perhaps as guided by state law, to deduct if appropriate.

—— **Case** ——

John Adams reported late for work on July 3, 1981. As this was his fourth tardiness in six months, the employer suspended him for the balance of the shift. Adams worked the next day, the 4th of July, and the day after. When he received his paycheck, he discovered that, while he had been paid for work on the 4th of July, he had not received holiday pay. He grieved. The employer cited the provisions of the labor agreement requiring that, in order to qualify for holiday pay, the employee is required to work both the scheduled day before and the day after the holiday. Clearly, Adams had not worked the full day before. Accordingly, the employer claimed the deduction of pay was appropriate.

Question and Comment

(1) *What should the decision be?*

While there is some split of opinion in this area, the better argument would be that the deduction of holiday pay was improper. At the heart of this question is the purpose of the contested provision. The language exists for the purpose of ensuring that employees do not improperly extend vacation periods. Often, days immediately before and after vacation days are times of high absenteeism. To counter this, companies and unions often agree to language designed to provide an incentive to show up. But in this case, the employee's absence was not the result of some improper extension of the vacation. Rather, it was the employer that decreed his absence on that day. It may be argued that the absence (suspension) would not have occurred had the employee reported for work in a timely fashion on July 3. Yet, the punishment for that infraction was a suspension for the balance of the shift. To impose an additional day's loss of pay would be extending the punishment beyond its intended impact.

A related problem often arises with respect to accrual of vacation over periods of suspension. Even when contracts premise the employee's entitlement to vacation accrual upon a "working" status, arbitrators have been troubled by whether the parties intended "working" to mean being on the employment rolls as opposed to being actually scheduled on duty during the days in question.

One may argue about the relative merits of the respective positions. Reasonably speaking, however, the parties should direct themselves with some specificity to this problem in the labor agreement. It is the parties and not the arbitrators that should be resolving questions of this sensitivity.

8

Holidays, Vacations, and Leaves

Holidays

Virtually all collective bargaining agreements provide for granting holidays. Unless the parties agree to the contrary, the employer is usually held to have the right to assign employees to work on holidays. Sometimes the parties negotiate certain time limits after which an employee may not be assigned to holiday work. Through the negotiation process, the parties also reach agreement on several aspects of pay for such time off including the number of holidays, amount of compensation for work performed on holidays, and eligibility for pay on unworked holidays.

Number and Selection of Holidays

The number of holidays negotiated by the parties has increased over the years until the majority of collective bargaining agreements now provide for 10 such holidays per year.[1] Beyond the traditional official federal and state holidays, parties frequently recognize holidays celebrated in their area.

---

[1] In 1979, 17 percent of all contracts had 12 or more holidays, with a maximum of 15, according to *Basic Patterns in Union Contracts* (Washington, D.C.: BNA Books, 1979), at 18.

They may even include holidays that reflect and accommodate the religious and/or racial makeup of the work force and the work requirements of the industry. In some contracts, the parties agree to holidays that are personal to the individual employee, such as his or her birthday.

The arbitrator is, of course, bound by the holidays negotiated by the parties. He or she cannot substitute his judgment or, indeed, that of the federal or state legislature, by mandating a holiday that the parties have omitted. It must be presumed they were aware of the available choices when they negotiated for certain holidays, and it is their selection of holidays that controls the neutral.

There are times when special holidays are mandated by government, such as occurred following the Kennedy assassination, or when a natural disaster motivates the announcement of a state holiday, as was the case in Massachusetts following the "Great Blizzard" of 1978. Although such holidays may relieve employees of the obligation to report to work on those days, they do not normally mandate that the employer make the days paid holidays. A number of arbitrators have faced situations where grieving employees seek compensation for the workday thus denied them. Most arbitrators hold that the unilateral creation of a holiday by the government, or even its allowance by the employer, does not automatically create holiday pay entitlement under the holiday provision of the agreement, although they may find that payment is justified under other clauses such as those covering reporting for work, availability of work, or guaranteed work weeks. However, absent specific language in the labor agreement, arbitrators will not infer a guarantee of work.

A somewhat different result might occur in the public sector where a declaration of a holiday by the head of state or local government (i.e., the governor or mayor) or the chief employer may be construed by an arbitrator as containing a commitment to compensate employees for the lost day of work which subordinate supervisors such as department heads are bound to respect and implement.

Often, contract language concerning holidays is ambiguous.

—— **Case** ——

The parties' agreement provides as follows:

New Years' Day   Labor Day
Washington's Birthday   Thanksgiving Day
Easter Sunday   Christmas Day
Memorial Day   And Two Religious Holidays
Fourth of July   of the Employee's Choice

The grievant, Brian Casey, takes off Yom Kippur and Good Friday. When questioned, he claims he is an atheist but is entitled to the two days' holiday pay nonetheless. He is denied pay for both days and grieves.

Questions and Comments

(1) *If you were the arbitrator, how would you rule?*

A "strict constructionist" might take the position that the parties provided for two religious holidays, that Yom Kippur and Good Friday are such, and that, absent a requirement that the grievant be of the faith involved, he or she would be entitled to take off the day with pay. That view would be bolstered by the more practical argument that the employer and the union negotiated for two extra days of holiday pay beyond the specified holidays and that it would be improper to deprive a nonbeliever of the economic benefit.

Another view might challenge the authenticity of the grievant's religious holiday claim. This view would hold that there is no inherent right to holiday pay, the provision is intended only to overcome the financial loss suffered by those for whom it is a religious observance, and that no holiday pay is due unless the religious holiday is actually observed.

(2) *Is it essential for an employee invoking a religious holiday to attend religious services in order to receive pay for the day? What if the foreman denied the religious holiday pay*

because he or she saw the employee at the race track on a claimed religious holiday?

Although arbitrators seek to apply the contract in conformity with the intent of the parties, they would probably not require attendance at religious services unless the contract so specified; for example, "employees may take a religious holiday for purposes of attending services." Obviously, in this sensitive area of religious expression, even one inclined to require that the time be actually devoted to religious observance would be loath to attempt to define the required form of worship. Even in the absence of contract language, protecting the exercise or nonexistence of religious beliefs is an area arbitrators are loath to enter, particularly when legal avenues are open to the parties for protection or enforcement of statutory freedoms of religious expression.

Thus, once an arbitrator reached the conclusion that an employee had a contractual basis for compensation for a religious holiday, most would not intrude into the area of policing how the employee spent the day.

Eligibility for Holiday Pay

If an employee works a scheduled holiday, he or she will normally be entitled to the standard wage or, if agreed upon, premium pay, in addition to holiday pay. To control absenteeism and protect against employees extending a holiday for personal convenience, employers frequently require the employee to work the scheduled workday before and after the holiday to be eligible for compensation for the holiday itself.

The arbitrator's judgment may be required in such cases to determine the eligibility of employees for holiday pay in terms of whether or not they worked the requisite scheduled day before and after. If the intent of such work-before-and-after clauses is to control absenteeism, it would follow that employees should be required to work their personally scheduled last day of work before and their personally scheduled first day after the holiday. If an employee is not among the crew scheduled for work on Saturday, July 2, it might be argued that he or she is ineligible for holiday pay on Monday, July 4. Such a result, however, would penalize the employee for nonattendance over which he or she had no control and permit the employer to rely upon scheduling quirks to deprive employees of their holiday pay entitlement. Unless the contract is explicit in requiring work on the actual day before the holidays, most arbitrators would find the requirement runs to the employee's schedule, for it is to deter absence on the *employee's* last scheduled day that the eligibility prerequisite is based.

Likewise, unless the contract is explicit in requiring a full day's work on such dates, arbitrators would generally look to whether the overall intent of the provision was met in the case of an employee who, because of illness, reported in tardy on the scheduled day before a holiday. Such an employee might qualify for the pay. The employee who punched in on time but then turned around and left work shortly thereafter might, by the same reasoning, be denied the pay.

A related issue arises in cases of holidays occurring during periods of layoff. The requirement of work before and/or after the layoff might still be invoked to grant holiday pay in case of a layoff for a week or two, but under the foregoing reasoning, an employee who worked his or her last scheduled day of work on January 1 and did not return to work for one year, would be entitled to all negotiated holidays. Here, arbitrators would be more likely to find that the goal of protecting an employee's expectancy of compensation that would have been received except for the creation of the holiday, is no longer applicable. Since an employee on layoff would have no expectation of work or income, that expectancy would be likewise applicable to holidays occurring during the period of extended absence, and thus, no compensation for such days would be in order.

The parties also usually anticipate the likelihood of some holidays falling on the weekend by providing for their observance on a Friday or a Monday. Absent clear language in the agreement to that effect, the arbitrator's determination might be guided by the statutes calling for Sunday holidays being celebrated on Monday or by the parties' past practice in handling prior weekend holidays. Problems in this area can be avoided by negotiating language that recognizes a state or federal day of observance for its own employees as controlling.

Most contracts anticipate the problem of holidays arising

during vacations by specifying whether or not employees will be compensated therefor, and whether or not they will be given a substitute day off. Arbitrators have been called upon to resolve conflicts between language which requires work "the day before and the day after a holiday" and language permitting holiday pay for holidays occurring during vacations. In such a dispute the intent of the work-before-and-after requirement is often held to be vitiated by the more specific requirement of holiday pay, even if the holiday occurs during a vacation—when the negotiators are presumed to have been aware that work on the day before and after the holiday would be unattainable. Although arbitrators in such a case would construe the "day" before and after the holiday as the day when the employee was able, i.e., scheduled to work, since the purpose of the day-before-and-after requirement is to avoid extending holidays by unjustified absences before or after. That goal is met when the employee works the day before and the day after his or her vacation. Most arbitrators would grant holiday pay for a holiday occurring during a vacation, for to do otherwise would place a premium on certain nonholiday weeks for vacations while penalizing those whose vacation dates happen to include holidays. The parties often provide in their agreements for such holiday benefits by granting an additional day off with pay, or by granting an additional day's pay, or leaving the choice up to the employee. Absent such specific language, the arbitrator would have the responsibility for fashioning an appropriate remedy for the holiday and/or holiday pay denial, probably opting for the additional day's pay in lieu of mandating another nonholiday day off.

Compensatory Time

Not all employees have the option of taking off holidays. Some enterprises and governmental units have round-the-clock operations that require employee attendance even on holidays. Unions, recognizing such requirements of service, frequently negotiate for compensatory time off, enabling employees who must work on the holiday to take off another nonholiday day with pay. Although there may be agreement that the holidays will be worked at the employee's regular rate of pay, there is often provision for some form of premium pay, in addition to the holiday pay. Wage payments may be escalated if the worked holiday falls on another premium day such as Sunday, but the parties may also limit the premium compensation to one set of premiums by inserting a provision barring the pyramiding of premium pay.

The parties adopt various rates of compensation for work performed on holidays, running from time-and-a-half to triple-time pay for that day. Questions frequently arise as to the obligation of the employee to work on holidays.

——— **Case** ———

The parties' agreement calls for July 4 as a holiday but the contract also provides that:

> If business requires, the employer may assign employees to work on holidays at double-time pay.

The supervisor directs Max Mirell to come in on the holiday saying that he wants to meet a sudden rush of orders before the July 15 deadline without having to work overtime. Mirell works the day but grieves the assignment and the fact he was paid only double time. He says he is entitled to double time for the holiday plus straight time for the day worked.

Questions and Comments

(1) *Should the arbitrator find the grievant entitled to double or triple his regular pay that day?*

If one assumes that an employee would receive regular pay for a holiday *not* worked, it should follow that he would receive additional pay for working the holiday. The question is whether the contract requires an additional straight- or double-time payment beyond the regular holiday pay.

The more compelling argument in this case is that, while holiday pay exists to compensate one who does not work, the above-cited clause was negotiated for the express purpose of establishing the rate for those who do. *Without* the clause, one who worked the holiday would receive straight-time pay (and holiday pay). The parties would hardly have negotiated a specific provision to accomplish the same goal.

(2) *Would you find the July 15 delivery deadline to meet the business requirement standards of the agreement?*

Most arbitrators would start with the standard that negotiated holidays are for employees to enjoy with their families, that the negotiated right to assign employee was restricted to business necessity, and that the burden is on the employer to establish that there was such a "requirement" in this case. The employer's case would be stronger if it showed that the holiday work was needed in addition to overtime. Most arbitrators would hold that avoidance of overtime is not valid grounds for infringement on the employee's right to a holiday.

(3) *Would the particular holiday make any difference?*

Probably not. If the arbitrator were to rely on the importance of a holiday with one's family, it would follow that the more family-oriented holidays would place a greater obstacle in the way of their erosion. Thus, work on a Christmas holiday might well dictate a greater showing of necessity than work on Armistice Day. But in so holding, the arbitrator may be ascribing varying weight to the respective holidays, reading into them values not specified in the contract or demonstrated in the provision's negotiated history.

(4) *How would you rule if the holiday fell on a Sunday and the parties' agreement provided that "any work performed on a Sunday will be compensated at double time"?*

Clearly a contractual ban on pyramiding would prohibit payment of the holiday *and* the Sunday pay. But in the absence of such a ban, the arbitrator would have to determine if the absence of a ban calls for payment of both benefits, which might be as high as quadruple pay. In making his or her determination, the arbitrator would be guided by the payment practice for work performed on prior Sunday holidays, by the evidence of what transpired in the negotiations for the two provisions, and by any prior arbitration awards or negotiating history dealing with payment of double fringe benefits such as holidays or vacations. Absent any evidence of intent to restrict pyramiding of pay, the grievant would be entitled to quadruple pay for the time worked.

Remedy

Since holidays are on fixed dates, an employee who follows an order to work on a holiday, then grieves, may be severely inconvenienced. He or she may have preferred not to have worked in order to be with his or her family. He or she may have made holiday plans at considerable cost. If the contract grants him or her the right to take the holiday off or if there is a finding that the employer ordered the employee to work after the contractual time unit had passed for such holiday work, there would be a question as to the remedy to which the employee is entitled. Remedy questions may also arise if the employee who worked the holiday without protest felt he or she was improperly compensated.

While it is the goal of arbitrators in formulating remedies to make employees whole for the loss and inconvenience they suffered in complying with an order that is later found to have been improper, it is not always possible to re-establish the *status quo ante*. Sometimes an arbitrator may permit the employee to take a subsitute day as a holiday. Arbitrators, and thus the successful grievant, are more likely limited in recovery to reimbursing financial losses and would be unlikely to go beyond their work place jurisdiction to compensate for the lost benefit that the grievant surrendered in obeying his supervisor's order to work now and grieve later.

——— Case ———

     Rebecca Sandman's 60th birthday on July 4 was to be celebrated by a family reunion with relatives coming from all over the country to join her. On July 2 she was advised by her employer that she was needed for work on that day. When she protested that she had other plans, she was told she would be disciplined for failing to report to work as ordered.

Questions and Comments

(1) *If she had taken the day off, been given a three-day suspension, and grieved, how would you, as the arbitrator, decide her case?*

     The issue in such a case is not the legitimacy of the work order, but rather the propriety of the disciplinary action taken against the grievant. The employer would be assumed to have the right to assign work on the holiday absent clear language to the contrary. If the evidence shows that she had been warned of the penalty for failing to work, such refusal would be viewed as insubordination, i.e., the refusal of a legitimate order, and therefor punishable pursuant to the established standards of progressive discipline.

     A different result might occur if there was a clear ban on such holiday work assignments and the supervisor so acknowledged. In that case the arbitrator might well find that the assignment was arbitrary and capricious and rule that although the grievant was generally obligated to follow the work orders of her supervisor, that responsibility would not run to following orders that the supervisor admitted were in explicit violation of the parties' agreement.

(2) *How would you rule if the grievant complied with the order, did work as directed, and then grieved for reimbursement of the money laid out for food and for long distance calls to relatives to cancel the reunion?*

Assuming there was no ban on the employer ordering such overtime, the arbitrator's decision would probably hinge on the timeliness of the holiday assignment and the propriety of selecting the grievant to work. If the evidence showed that she was the employee properly scheduled for the holiday work and that she was given the appropriate notice of her assignment, then her claim would undoubtedly be denied.

But if the evidence showed that she was not correctly scheduled to work on the holiday or that she had been given less notice of the assignment than required in the contract, then the arbitrator would undoubtedly find that she was correct in grieving. It is unlikely that an arbitrator would award reimbursement for the consequent costs of the improper assignment. A more likely remedy would be the granting of a paid substitute day off.

(3) *Would your decision as an arbitrator be affected by whether or not she was actually needed that day?*

Most arbitrators would not second-guess a reasonable business judgment of the employer as to whether she was required to work on that holiday. Even if there were such language, and the arbitrator found that the grievant was not required for the holiday work, it is unlikely that the remedy would be any more than a substitute holiday. If the employer had the right to schedule Ms. Sandman on that holiday, its use of the grievant would not be considered relevant.

Vacations

Even before collective bargaining, employers generally provide for vacation, usually gearing the length of the vacation to the employee's length of service. The advent of collective bargaining will result either in the codification of pre-existing practices or in negotiated changes that are incorporated into the parties' agreement. The most frequent subject matters for grievances in this area are eligibility, scheduling, and compensation for vacations.

Eligibility. Vacation entitlement is usually dependent upon certain work requirements:

(1) The employee has completed a defined term of continuous service with the employer.
(2) A certain number of hours, days, weeks, or months of actual work have been performed in the vacation year.
(3) The employee be available on a particular date triggering the start of the vacation period.

In addition, the length of the individual's vacation is usually tied to his or her length of service.

 **Case**

The parties' agreement provides that

Paid vacation will be provided to those employees with one or more years of continuous service as of May 31 and who have worked three-fourths of the work year.

Ethan Larson, the grievant, has been with the company for nine years and would normally be entitled to three weeks of vacation. He was out of work, receiving full pay, due to a work-related injury for half the year, and was denied his paid vacation. He grieved.

Questions and Comments

(1) *If you were the arbitrator, how would you rule?*

The fact that Larson was not available for work for half the year, and thus had not actually worked the requisite three-fourths of the year, means that, by definition, he is not eligible for the negotiated paid vacation. Yet, the reason for his absence was a work-related injury, one that was beyond his control, one for which the employer has assumed financial responsibility. Since it was clearly an approved leave of absence, and since he was treated financially by the employer as though he *had* worked the time, some arbitrators would find that the grievant had constructively met the eligibility requirements for paid vacation. Other arbitrators, however, applying a strict construction to the term "worked three-fourths of the year," would find that by being physically unavailable to do the work, Larson would not be entitled to paid vacation under the contract.

If the half year was a voluntary leave, or perhaps even an uncompensated not-work-related injury, then there would be greater uniformity among arbitrators in denying the three-week paid vacation. Although a few arbitrators might seek to award the grievant half his vacation entitlement for the period he actually did work, most would probably find that by voluntarily taking off the half year, Larson failed to meet the threshold contractual requirement for *any* paid vacation.

(2) *Would Larson be entitled to paid vacation if he had worked until April 15 and then been placed on layoff status through June 30?*

The contractual requirement calls for work for three-fourths of the year, which Larson had completed prior to going on layoff status. He had fully accrued his vacation entitlement and since vacation is an earned benefit rather than a reward or a bonus for reaching a target calendar date, most arbitrators would find the grievant entitled to the paid vacation following his return to work or, if he remains on layoff, at least to payment of the amount he would have received had he continued to work.

(3) *If Larson had been terminated for insubordination in October, grieved the termination, and been subsequently reinstated by an arbitrator "with full back pay" in May, would he be entitled to his paid vacation?*

An arbitration award that found the employee innocent of the charges against him would usually mandate that the grievant be made whole for all benefits improperly denied him. Thus, unless the arbitrator found the grievant partly at fault and imposed some measure of penalty, the intent would be to wipe the slate clean of that offense and of the penalty improperly imposed because of it. Under this approach, he would receive a paid vacation.

A more troublesome problem arises when the arbitrator finds that the grievant was entitled to some discipline, but determines that the termination penalty was excessive and that the employee should be reinstated with a lesser penalty. If that penalty should have been a one-week, two-week, or even a month suspension, then the grievant would be entitled to be made whole for all the additional benefits that were denied him, including lost wages and any vacation to which he would have been entitled had the employer initially imposed the penalty that the arbitrator later found appropriate.

The greatest confusion arises in cases of reinstatement without back pay. If the intent thereof is to provide the employee with one last chance, the arbitrator is, in effect, stating that the employee was properly provided with a disciplinary penalty from the date of his discharge until the date of his reinstatement. Under such a theory, the grievant would be entitled only to such paid vacation as would have been vested at the time of his termination.

Scheduling

Management is generally considered to retain the right to schedule vacations as a facet of its right to assign and schedule work. Even without negotiated restrictions on that right, the employer may seek to accommodate the wishes of its employees. The parties may negotiate the employees' right to select a vacation period in order of seniority, but even that choice is often subject to being overruled by the staffing requirements of the employer.

The parties may also negotiate to permit employees to take vacations at any time of the year or may agree to restrict the vacation scheduling to a fixed period, for example, between June 1 and October 1. They may even agree to have all employees take their vacations at one time by scheduling a vacation shutdown. Sometimes they agree to permit accumulation of vacation entitlement in whole or in part into subsequent years to provide for longer but less frequent vacation periods.

—— **Case** ——

The pertinent provision of the parties' agreement reads as follows:

Vacation periods will be awarded by seniority. Every effort will be made to assure that the preferences are protected.

Laura Marshall was scheduled to take her vacation during the first two weeks of August. In mid-July her supervisor informed Marshall that a rush order required her to postpone her vacation for three weeks. She worked as required but filed a grievance seeking reimbursement of a $300 deposit she made on a vacation rental which she had to forfeit.

Questions and Comments

(1) *If you were the arbitrator, how would you rule?*

Although the first sentence of the contract provision does say "vacations will be awarded," that mandatory language runs only to the requirement that such vacation allotment will be made by seniority. There is no question that Marshall's assignment of the first two weeks of August was made pursuant to that provision, but the language does not make that assignment immutable. The second sentence makes that clear. It obligates the employer to accommodate the employees' selection of vacation period. But, by its terms, it does not guarantee that the selected dates will be ensured. It contains an implied reservation to alter that schedule if the needs of the employer require the presence of the employee during the scheduled vacation period.

Thus, if the employer has a rush order that requires the grievant's presence, he may schedule him or her for work and postpone the vacation. Most arbitrators would accept the employer's right to alter the planned vacation for its production requirements. They would probably read into the second sentence a standard of reasonableness. Thus, if it were shown that the employer acted in pique against the grievant or that the work could reasonably have been done by its regularly scheduled work force, most arbitrators would conclude that the employer had not made "every effort to assure" that the vacation preference was protected and would find that the vacation postponement was improper.

(2) *If the arbitrator found the vacation postponement improper, what should be the remedy?*

Consistent with the precept that the arbitrator's authority is to rectify employment inequities, most arbitrators would find the consequent damage claim of $300 to be without merit and would award the grievant an additional vacation period.

(3) *How would you rule if grievant refused to take the postponed dates and opted in her grievance for a double vacation next year, where the contract contained no provision for accumulation of vacation?*

Unless the contract provided for "banking" vacation time, it would be inappropriate for the arbitrator to award it, for in so doing, the arbitrator would be rewriting the parties' agreement. But it would be equally harsh to rule that the grievant, by declining to take the delayed vacation, had waived her right to any vacation that year. Since the grievant would probably not have come to the arbitration step until many months after the summer vacation season, the arbitrator might well rule that the grievant is entitled to the money for the vacation she passed up, but not to a double vacation with pay in the upcoming period.

Compensation

Vacation pay is generally held to be an accrued benefit rather than merely a "bonus" for a years' work performance. The intent of most vacation provisions is to assure that the employee will be given the appropriate vacation time off with the same pay he or she would have received if working during that period. Vacation compensation is usually based on the employee's straight-time hourly earnings, omitting overtime and shift differentials, to which the employee would have been entitled if at work. In some agreements, the parties specify that such compensation shall be equal to average weekly earnings during the year or to earnings during a particular pay period. There may also be agreement to pay shift differentials, average overtime earnings, and even wage increases coming due during the employee's vacation period.

Interpretative disputes do arise as to proper compensation. For example, if the contract called for "straight-time earnings" and the employee's compensation excluded shift differentials, an employee may grieve that exclusion. If there is ambiguity in the contract, the arbitrator would consider the prior practice of the parties in paying such benefits, their negotiating history, if any, the contractual references as to what is included in straight-time earnings, and the basic intent of the vacation compensation provision to protect the employee's receipt of normally expected levels of compensation during vacation periods.

For employees on layoffs, sick leave, leave of absence, newly on retirement, or indeed, those who have quit or who have been terminated, there remains the question of their compensation entitlement. If the employee has not met the eligibility requirements prior to departure from active employment, there may be a dispute over the amount of vacation due. Many arbitrators, treating vacation pay as an earned benefit rather than a bonus, would provide a pro rata portion of the earned vacation pay for returning employees or for all employees on a plant closing, unless barred from doing so by the parties' agreement.

Leaves

In addition to holidays and vacations, employers have also granted employees individual days off or periods of leave when outside affairs, which the employer deemed justified, required the employee's attendance during normal working hours.

The right to take such leaves is normally dependent upon acquiescence of the employer, although permission generally must not be unreasonably withheld. Grievances frequently arise on the question of advance request for the leave taking, entitlement to such leave, and the question of compensation therefor.

Personal Leave

Most collective bargaining agreements provide paid leave for personal affairs that cannot be handled during nonworking hours. The provisions range from a right to take such leave without explaining the reason, to an identification of the general reason for the time taken (personal, family business, legal, etc.), to a specific explanation of the day's use, and ultimately, to the right of the employer to grant such a day or days off at the employer's discretion.

Unions usually seek to have total control over such days retained within the employees' discretion to protect their rights to privacy in matters affecting after-hours life. The employer, however, is often anxious to include in the provision some protection against abuse and unwarranted use of such paid leave days and to assure that the day is being taken to accomplish personal activities that, in fact, cannot be done during off-duty hours. These diverse views give rise to many disputes that find their way to arbitration.

—— Case ——

The parties' agreement provides that

Employees shall be entitled to two days of paid personal leave for business, family, or personal matters that cannot be taken care of at other times.

Barbara Chambers informed her supervisor that she was taking one day for personal reasons. When he asked what the reason was, she replied that it was "personal." The supervisor denied the leave, Chambers was allowed to take the day off without pay, and subsequently grieved to attain the lost day's pay.

Questions and Comments

(1) *If you were the arbitrator, how would you rule?*

The language of the parties' agreement does set forth three categories for which paid personal leave days may be taken. In that sense it merely identifies the generic areas of authorized leave. There is nothing in the cited contract language that either restricts the employer's right to inquire as to the purpose for the leave or that protects the employee from being required to make such an explanation.

The employer is entitled to some assurance that the paid day is not being taken for a frivolous reason, yet it is not entitled to such a detailed explanation of the planned activities as would constitute an invasion of the employee's right of privacy. Thus, the arbitrator would probably hold that the employer was entitled to a more detailed explanation than the mere reply of "personal business." The question of where the line of inquiry is to be drawn is a fine one. Most arbitrators would find that the employer's needs were met by a response such as, "I have to be in court at 10 a.m.," and that any further probing to ascertain the reason for the court appearance would be unwarranted. Note, however, that if the employee can prove at arbitration the leave was, indeed, for a valid personal matter, the grievance should be granted.

(2) *If the contract stated, "The employee need only identify which of the reasons the leave is to be used for . . . ," could the employer properly deny the leave if the grievant merely cited "personal business"?*

The addition of the language quoted here does protect the employee from excessive inquiry into the reason for an absence but also opens the door to greater abuse of leave days and handicaps the employer in the policing of the leave-taking system. Yet, the employer agreed to that language and, absent actual observance of the employees' activities on the day off, the only remedy for the employer is to seek more favorable language during the next contract negotiations.

(3) *If the employer learned that the grievant was observed at the race track on a "personal business" day off, and imposed a two-day suspension which was grieved and appealed to arbitration, how would you rule?*

If one begins with the assumption that "personal business" was meant by the parties to be more than a holiday, mere observation of the grievant at the race track is not per se proof of abuse of personal leave but would amount to a prima facie showing of abuse, placing the burden of response on the employee. The grievant might prove she took the leave for a 10 a.m. court appearance which ended at 1 p.m., too late to return to work, and so she went to the track. But, if the employee is unwilling or unable to substantiate the authenticity of her taking the personal business day, then she must suffer the penalty for abuse of the personal leave day benefit. Of course, she might establish that she has long maintained a racing stable on Long Island near her job, that she had not wanted it to interfere with her work duties, and that she believed that taking a personal leave day to watch her prize horse compete for the Triple Crown was an activity she could not have done during afterwork hours.

Long-Term Leaves

Long-term leaves of absence may be for certain specified reasons (military service, union affairs, etc.) in which case it may have been agreed that the leaves "shall be granted." In other circumstances, management may retain full discretion to grant or deny the request, assuming that denials are not unreasonably withheld.

Disputes often arise over the issue of reasonableness of both the requests and the denials. Unless there is an established precedent for handling these issues, most arbitrators will assert that the union has the burden of establishing that the employer's denial or restrictions on the taking of such leave was unjust or unreasonable.

Sometimes the arbitral issue focuses on the grievant's claim for return to the position held at the commencement of the leave. Unless the parties have negotiated language governing re-entry into employment or unless there is evidence of a controlling practice, the union has the burden of establishing that the employer's action or refusal to reinstate to the requested position was unreasonable. A related problem is the failure of the person on leave of absence to return to work within the stipulated time period, leaving the employer to consider the employee as a voluntary quit.

In the case of academic employment, the sabbatical leave of absence may be governed by contract language specifying a certain number or percentage of the teaching force to be eligible for sabbatical in a given year and governing the amount of full or partial compensation to be paid to teachers during such leave.

—— Case ——

The parties' agreement provides:

An applicant for sabbatical shall submit a planned program for the sabbatical year which will improve teaching skills on return to the system. The employer will select the three senior applicants whose program of study will contribute most to improved academic performance on their return to the system. Those selected will be paid one-half their earnings for the year.

Sam is a 14-year teacher of manual arts in high school who has enough seniority to apply for a sabbatical year from his school system. He is the most senior of the four applicants for three sabbaticals that year and seeks to hold a full-time position in a local lumber yard. The superintendent selects the three employees junior to Sam, asserting that since their programs were for academic research and degree improvement, they better met the needs of the system. Sam filed a grievance which was appealed to arbitration.

Questions and Comments

(1) *If you were the arbitrator, how would you rule?*

The parties' contract relies on seniority as the governing criterion, provided that the proposed programs of the applicants meet the goal of "improved academic competence." It mandates that the employer will select the three senior applicants if the conditions are met. Although some arbitrators might hold that only enrollment in academic programs during the year is suitable for meeting the conditions of the contract, others would probably recognize the limited academic options open to a teacher of manual arts and find that the term "academic" does not require enrollment in a course of study. Rather, it should be read to mean the enrichment of the teacher's capabilities to contribute to the academic competence of the school system. It would be necessary to determine if the employment Sam was seeking would in fact contribute to the improvement of his teaching competence on his return to work. Mere employment in a lumber yard might not improve his teaching skills, but employment as a technical consultant on do-it-yourself building projects sponsored by the lumber company might fulfill the contractual standards on an equal or better basis than a math teacher, for instance, pursuing a master's degree in social studies or a foreign language. If the arbitrator found that Sam's program would make him a better teacher on his return to the system, his grievance might well be sustained.

(2) *If the employer granted Sam the sabbatical but refused to provide him any compensation because he was entering a full-time job, and he grieved, how would you rule?*

The contract language is explicit in providing half pay to those on sabbatical. Thus, if Sam is awarded the sabbatical, even if taking a full-time job, he would appear to be entitled to the additional half pay. On the other hand, the employer might argue that such extra compensation was not the intent of the parties, that such would constitute unjust enrichment for Sam, and that the extra half pay should not be provided. Most arbitrators would, nevertheless, implement the clear terms of the parties' agreement.

(3) *Would the employer be justified in withholding payment of the half salary for all three until the end of the sabbatical year?*

Although the contract is silent on the matter of how payment of the half compensation is to be made, there is clearly no provision for withholding payment until the end of the year and, presumably, there is no contractual or past practice requirement of a successful conclusion of the sabbatical before receiving the half salary. To the contrary, the only portion of the time span mentioned in connection with compensation is the reference to selection. Since the intent of the parties was presumably to permit teachers to pursue their programs with receipt of one-half of "their regular earnings," it would be more reasonable for payments to be made on the same schedule as if they were at their regular teaching duties. This is one area in which the silence of the parties' agreement has to be fleshed out by the arbitrator using standards of reasonableness.

Funeral Leave

Most collective bargaining agreements provide for funeral leave. The negotiated issues are the categories of individuals (usually relatives) for which the leave may be invoked and the duration of the leave. The intent behind the provision is to relieve the employee of work responsibilities during a period of mourning and family grief. Some agreements specify that the employee must attend the funeral to receive the paid leave, some vary according to the distance which must be traveled to the funeral, and some require proof of death. In specifying the categories of individuals whose death triggers entitlement to the leave, the parties tend to restrict the categories to relatives and, in some cases, to relatives living in the household. Entitlement to the leave is occasionally extended to close companions in nonmarital relationships or to step- or foster-parent or foster-child relationships.

Arbitrators are often called upon to resolve questions of entitlement to such leave regarding duration thereof, the scope of activities permitted during the leave, and the closeness of the relationship.

―――― **Case** ――――

The pertinent language in the parties' agreement reads as follows:

In the event of the death of a parent . . . an employee shall be entitled to three days of funeral leave.

Rebecca advised her supervisor on May 1 that her father died and that she wished to take three days of funeral leave from May 2 to 4 under the above provision. The leave was granted but thereafter the supervisor learned that the parent died on April 15 while on safari in Africa, that the grievant did not learn of the demise until May 1, and that the body was not returned to the United States until May 10. The company deducts the three days' pay from the grievant's next paycheck, giving rise to this grievance which was appealed to arbitration.

Questions and Comments

(1) *If you were the arbitrator, how would you rule?*

Most arbitrators hold to the view that funeral leave is not an absolute guarantee of time off in the event of a parent's death. Rather, they would hold that the purpose of such leave is to provide employees a reasonable period of time off to attend the funeral of such family members as are specified in the leave provision. Since there was no funeral on the days taken off for the funeral leave, some arbitrators would hold that invocation of the funeral leave provision at that time was inappropriate, particularly since the body was not returned to the United States until May 10. They might, however, allow the leave at *that* time for a delayed funeral or the like. Clearly, this is an area where substantial flexibility is appropriate. If the evidence showed there was a memorial service on May 3, or that the grievant was busy during the three days arranging for shipment of the body and/or funeral, then the arbitrator might well find the three original "funeral leave" days justified and sustain the grievance. Although some arbitrators might construe funeral leave narrowly to require that a funeral or memorial service be held during the three days off, others would construe the clause more liberally as bereavement leave, recognizing that learning of the death of a parent would involve a period of bereavement and inability to properly attend to one's work duties. Although the employer would have the burden of showing that the claim for funeral leave was unjustified or at least untimely, grievant could meet that burden by showing that the impact of the overseas death was just as great, or perhaps greater, than if the father had died at home.

(2) *Assuming the death in question happened in the employee's home town, and in "timely" fashion, but that the individual was a stepfather rather than a natural father, would you then find the grievant entitled to the three days' leave?*

Although the contract specifies father, it does not exclude stepfather. It would be difficult to deny such leave if the evidence shows that the stepfather was the only father the grievant had known or if there was no evidence that a natural father existed. But if the evidence shows that grievant's natural father was also alive and had a close relationship with his daughter, one might conclude that, while she could utilize three days, she would do so only once.

Sick Leave

Employers have sought to regulate attendance problems created by absence due to illness by making available unilaterally or through contract negotiation a certain number of days of sick leave that employees may use without loss of pay or other penalty. In administering such a program, the employer may establish certain administrative procedures for invoking sick leave and for policing the legitimacy of its usage. It may require evidence of illness in all or only selected cases of absenteeism. It may require medical examination by its own or the employee's physician. It may subject the absent employee to unannounced inspection visits to determine the authenticity of a questioned absence.

In all these efforts to control the frequency and extent of absence due to illness, the employer faces the risk of challenge by the employee on questions of fact of illness as well as questions as to the propriety of the employer's policing activity. Many of these cases find their way to the arbitrators who will endorse the employer's right to impose administrative procedures on the use of sick leave but who will also determine whether such procedures were reasonable per se or reasonably invoked in a particular fact situation.

Maternity Leave

Related to the issue of sick leave is the employee's access to leave for childbirth and, on occasion, for child rearing. Entitlement to the former is often determined by the employer's sickness and accident insurance. Inasmuch as the 1978 Pregnancy Discrimination Act[2] prohibits employment discrimination because of "pregnancy, childbirth, or related medical conditions," a number of arbitration cases arise over conflict between the parties' negotiated disability leave provisions and the perceived guarantees of the statute. Although the ultimate resolution of issues of compliance with the statute rests within the purview of the courts rather than the arbitrator, there are a number of arbitrators who feel it is a part of their contractual responsibility to attempt to resolve such conflicts in their opinions. Indeed, the parties' agreement may even contain provisions mandating that the contract be interpreted or applied in conformity with existing external federal and/or state law. In such cases the arbitrator, although still subject to review and possible reversal by the courts of proper jurisdiction, may have the contractual duty to fulfill the responsibility of statutory interpretation that was required by the parties' negotiated agreement.

Without delving into the questions of arbitrators' standards in dealing with issues of external law, which is covered in Chapter 3 of this volume, we should note that there are still

---

[2]42 U.S.C. §2000e(k), 92 Stat. 2076 (1978).

strictly contractual issues that arise in arbitration on the question of childbirth leave.

——— **Case** ———

The parties' collective bargaining agreement for many years provided that the employer would make a lump sum payment to cover hospitalization costs of childbirth, the amount increasing in each successive contract. The employer arranged unilaterally with its insurance carrier to provide the funds for such payments. Shortly after the passage of the Pregnancy Discrimination Act, the company was advised by its insurance carrier that since the policy only provides for 80 percent coverage for male hospitalization it will no longer pay the full amount of hospitalization for childbirth up to the negotiated lump sum figure. A few weeks later, when Sarah applied for the contractual $500 to pay for her hospital bill during childbirth, she was sent a check for 80 percent thereof, or $400, giving rise to a grievance which is appealed to arbitration.

Questions and Comments

(1) *If you were the arbitrator, how would you rule?*

Unquestionably, some arbitrators would take it upon themselves to interpret the parties' agreement to pay the lump sum in light of the statutory requirement of equal treatment for males and females in disability cases such as childbirth, perhaps going so far as to restructure the contractual commitment to bring it into conformity with their understanding of the statute. Most arbitrators would probably not rule on the legal propriety of the lump sum payment for females hospitalized for childbirth and instead would confine their opinion and decision to the question of the employer's seeking to amend his contractual commitment in light of the reduced financial authorization by the insurance carrier. Unless the parties' agreement on the lump sum payment contained language making the payment thereof conditional upon the employer receiving such amounts from its insurance carrier or unless the insurance coverage itself were viewed as a condition precedent of payment of the lump sum, most arbitrators would find that the employer had made a commitment to that $500 reserving to itself the problem of funding such payment.

(2) *Would your answer differ if the employer's negotiator offered unrefuted testimony that during negotiations she or he said that the payment of the stipend depended on the employer's ability to secure insurance coverage therefor?*

When the contract language contains a clear provision for lump sum payment in the event of hospitalization, it is unlikely that an arbitrator would find such language sufficiently ambiguous to open the door to consideration of the parties' intent during negotiations. Rather, the arbitrator might conclude that if the employer intended the lump sum payment to be dependent upon insurance coverage, it was incumbent on the employer to so specify in the contract itself or, at the very least, in a signed letter of agreement. Having failed to secure such a safeguard, it would follow that the employer is bound by the commitment as set forth in the agreement it signed—for the full lump sum payment.

(3) *If, at the end of the two-month leave, Sarah's physician submits a letter stating she is not yet fit to return to work, and the employer's physician determines, after an examination, that she is fit to return to work, but she refuses to return, how would you rule on her request for continued disability payments?*

Unless the parties have negotiated a provision authorizing the employee's physician or the employer's physician as the controlling authority in determining when an employee shall return to work, the conflict between physicians may create a dispute which comes before the arbitrator for resolution. Some arbitrators will suggest to the parties that they designate a mutually acceptable physician to arbitrate the impasse; others will select an independent physician and have him or her make the judgment based upon the record or examination of the grievant (with the acquiescence of the parties). But most arbitrators will make the determination on their own, exercising their best judgment on the basis of the documentary evidence and testimony of the conflicting physicians. Entitlement to child-rearing leave, as with any other form of long-term leave, is often a matter of managerial discretion. The parties do, on occasion, negotiate eligibility, frequency, duration, and access to prior position on return to work.

9

Job Evaluation

Job evaluation provisions are by no means universal in collective bargaining agreements. Nor could one hope to provide more than a brief sketch of such systems in the space allotted here. Nevertheless, these provisions are often significant to the parties' contractual relationship yet they are rarely discussed.

The purpose of job evaluation systems is to attempt to establish a method by which various classifications in a production facility may be assigned wage rates. As will be discussed below, most systems generate a given number of "points" to be assigned a job. The points are then translated into job grades to which wage rates are assigned. In theory, the job grades are determined more by application of the evaluation formula than by bargaining, while collective bargaining is relegated to the process of establishing applicable rates for each grade.

In practice, however, questions often arise as to whether a job is properly evaluated. This can arise in the case of a new job—one that has been created, but was previously unranked—or a changed job wherein essential duties or equipment has been modified.

Job evaluation, or job classification systems, range in sophistication. A relatively basic system, employed for the most part in small enterprises, simply takes an overview of the various classifications. Jobs are ranked on the basis of least demanding to most demanding. This system relies heavily on subjective judgments as to the nature of the jobs and may suffer from the fact that dissimilar classifications are being com-

pared. A job classification system, such as has been historic-
ally utilized by the federal government, establishes a general
schedule to which jobs are compared then graded. Grades are
defined by the so-called government service (GS) levels, and
standards are developed for each grade. Then, job descriptions
are compared against the grades to see at which level a job
should be compensated. This system places heavy reliance on
written job descriptions and a certain margin for error inasmuch as job descriptions can be drafted to conform to the
standards. There is some indication that the federal government is moving toward a factor evaluation, or "point" system,
discussed below, which is generally regarded as the most sophisticated evaluation process.

Most job evaluation systems reflect the programs developed in the 1930s by the National Metal Trades Association
(NMTA) and the National Electrical Manufacturers' Association (NEMA). The general approach is to scrutinize a series of
attributes of an individual job, assigning points for each at-
tribute, and then totaling the points to arrive at a job grade.
Normally, 10 or 11 categories are reviewed. For example, a
wage evaluation system now utilized in the aluminum industry
establishes the following 11 "factors":

(1) Related (academic) knowledge
(2) Job knowledge and experience
(3) Manual skill
(4) Responsibility for loss
(5) Responsibility for the performance of others
(6) Responsibility for safety of others
(7) Mental demand
(8) Physical demand
(9) Surroundings
(10) Hazards
(11) Responsibility for production

Each of the above-mentioned factors is composed of a series of
"levels" wherein points are assigned depending on the relative degree of difficulty. As an example, Factor 1 is defined by
the parties in general terms as follows:

> Refers to the academic or technical knowledge required
> for the performance of the job. Consider the type of knowl-
> edge that normally is obtained from academic training

and schooling, but which may be obtained through self-study, as contrasted to that which usually is obtained through practical experience.

Within that factor, there exists a series of levels:

Factor Level
Weight

Level 1. Work requiring understanding verbal in- 2.0
structions, reading and writing simple
material, counting and recording simple
data, and using simple gauges.

Level 2. Work requiring reading and writing with 5.3
ease, using micrometers, and other comparable adjustable gauges and measuring devices, making simple arithmetic
calculations, using operating charts
and manuals, and using prints, sketches,
and written data to determine simple
specifications.

Level 3. Work requiring complex calculation us- 8.6
ing fractions, decimals, and percentages
for reports or tabulations. Work involving interpretation of detailed prints and
written specifications.

Level 4. Work requiring thorough knowledge of 11.9
trade or other work involving the use of
shop mathematics, complex formulas,
and blueprints.

Level 5. Work requiring analysis and solving 15.0
technical or trade problems involving
formulas, handbooks, and interpretation
of complex diagrammatic or mechanical
drawings. Requires thorough knowledge
of current technical developments in the
field.

Note that each factor level is assigned a "weight" in terms of points. Once jobs have been ranked in each level of each factor, the points are totaled and a wage rate applied, depending on accumulated points.

Even where the evaluation systems are similar, parties differ dramatically in their application. Some, for example, make continued reference to the "level language" within a factor to seek proper placement of a job. Others use the level language solely to establish an original rank ordering of jobs. Once a hierarchy of jobs has been created within the individual factors, level language is disregarded for later ranking purposes. Instead, the parties evaluate new or changed jobs solely by comparison to existing classifications. Still other groups utilize a "benchmark" system, wherein certain key jobs are agreed upon as exhibiting various characteristics; comparison classifications are held up to the benchmark jobs to see where, in the relative hierarchy, they should be placed.

The role of the arbitrator varies in job evaluation disputes. Some parties empower the arbitrator to decide all aspects of the dispute. Thus, the task is to review the job, establish the appropriate ranking, then assign a wage grade to establish the appropriate compensation level. In other cases, the arbitrator's authority is somewhat more limited. He or she is empowered to perform the evaluation function in terms of ranking the job. However, the parties are thereafter responsible for the purely mechanical task of assigning the job grade. This distinction is premised on the assumption that any considerations of salary levels are irrelevant in terms of the arbitrator's evaluation functions. There are also parties who restrict the arbitrator's role to the question of whether the job was properly ranked. The arbitrator may find that it was improperly ranked, but he or she has no authority to establish an appropriate ranking, let alone a wage rate. Instead, the matter is simply referred to the parties for further negotiation.

Despite the reliance on factors, levels, points, and an attempt by the parties to systematize the matter, job evaluation remains as much an art as a science. What is the impact, in terms of ranking, of across-the-board increased (or decreased) production? On the one hand, certain elements measured by the system, such as physical demand, may be meaningfully affected. On the other hand, it may also be that there is an impact on all jobs in the plant. If parties operate under a relative ranking system, such obvious change may result in no reranking. What is to be made of the slow but steady changes that occur over a period of years? From a theoretical standpoint, these changes must be evaluated and acknowledged. Practically speaking, it may be difficult or impossible to record them or to invest the time and money to litigate them at each step. Considering these, and other realities of the job evaluation system, it is apparent that careful, attentive administration by both parties is essential to the viability of the process.

The evidence in a job evaulation case is directed to familiarize the arbitrator not only with the job at stake, but also the evaluation system itself and any other comparison classifications or definitions that may be relevant. Accordingly, hearings in these matters may be considered more complex than, for example, the routine discharge or discipline case.

Ideally, there should be little dispute about the required job functions. Supervisors and bargaining unit employees should not differ significantly on what is being done, although it is often the case that recollections will differ as to what may have been required over past periods of time. Often, companies and unions seek to agree on job descriptions, wherein the primary functions, duties, and equipment are set forth. These descriptions serve as aids in describing the job but will rarely be sufficiently comprehensive to describe each and every detail of the required work. Thus, in addition to the testimony of witnesses, it is important for the arbitrator to view the job itself. Plant visitations will be scheduled for this purpose.

Overall, evaluation systems may provide effective mechanisms for ensuring, to whatever extent possible, objective reviews of new and changed jobs. They serve, as well, to narrow the potential scope of negotiations; once the relative positioning of the jobs has been accomplished, it remains only for the parties to bargain over the applicable wage rates.

10

Future of the Labor Agreement

At the Second Annual Meeting of the National Academy of Arbitrators in 1949, George W. Taylor said that "[c]ontrary to the views of many arbitrators, grievance settlement is not simply a process of contract interpretation."[1] Professor Taylor saw the vitality of the arbitration process as dependent upon its being accepted as an extension of the collective bargaining function. It was neither exclusively a mediation process nor a judicial process. Rather, the arbitrator was to be seen as an important agent in the shaping, where necessary, of labor relations policy. Taylor endorsed the concept of an impartial chairman, who would sit as the neutral member of a tripartite panel on a continuous basis, perhaps for the term of a contract. That individual would acquire an ongoing understanding of the industry and would seek to mediate grievance cases when possible, but would also vote to break a deadlock when it was not possible. Taylor noted, however, that there are instances where either party would be unwilling to assume the various risks in having a third-party participate in making vital collective bargaining decisions as an impartial chairman. Under such circumstances, he recommended the umpire system—a sole arbitrator appointed for the term of the contract who would take no

---

[1]Taylor, "Effectuating the Labor Contract Through Arbitration," in *The Profession of Labor Arbitration*, Selected Papers from the First Seven Annual Meetings of the National Academy of Arbitrators (Washington, D.C.: BNA Books, 1957), at 21.

part in forging labor relations policy. Taylor's words are significant:

> "Although common sense and compromise can be freely exercised by the parties in the earlier steps of the grievance procedure in an effort to hammer out a meeting of minds, much less latitude is possessed by the 'outsider' under the pure Umpire system. It is the umpire's job to rule 'legalistically' on the contract as written and on the evidence as adduced, irrespective of whether or not the result, in the umpire's judgment, is sound from an industrial relations standpoint. If the decision is difficult or impossible to live with, then the parties will be made aware of the urgency of compromising their difficulties and of avoiding arbitration."[2]

Professor Taylor saw the umpire system as effective to the extent it induced agreements at the earlier stages of the grievance procedure; i.e., to the extent the parties did not have to actually utilize the system for final decisions:

> "But if large numbers of cases are arbitrated, the basic purpose of the system will not be achieved, and the program will inevitably fail. Submission of a large volume of issues to an umpire evidences an inability of the parties peacefully to resolve their differences. A backlog of extremely difficult problems may be built up for treatment when a new contract is negotiated. And grievances unacceptably handled during the term can't be satisfactorily dealt with in contract negotiations."[3]

These were the words of the man whom many regard, properly so, as one of the several founders of modern-day labor arbitration. If one compares his observations to the present-day state of grievances resolution, there is considerable cause for concern.

As noted in Chapter 3, at least one commentator has reviewed the increasing impact of public laws on private processes and concluded that the golden age of arbitration is at an end. Surely this is not the case in terms of work for arbitrators. The prospect of private dispute resolution is, for the moment at least, bright. But the nature of the procedures has, indeed, changed dramatically, and the overall prognosis in terms of maintaining an effective internal dispute settlement procedure must be guarded.

The very existence of this book, with its emphasis on con-

---

[2]*Id.* at 38.
[3]*Id.*

tract interpretation and its significant chapters on interpretation techniques, including the impact of external law, is some evidence that times have changed. Ad hoc arbitration, as opposed to umpireships, is the way of the present. Individual arbitrators stand less chance of becoming intimately familiar with one particular industry for, of necessity, they move from shop to shop. New arbitrators tend to become schooled, if at all, by exposure to a series of unrelated cases and a variety of arbitrators. The opportunities today to "apprentice" in the company of one individual immersed in a particular industry are rare. Companies and unions are paying increasing attention to external laws and the pressure of fair representation challenges such that disputes that have their origin in the work place may not necessarily be fully and finally settled in that same forum. Not all of these developments are disadvantageous. Ad hoc systems tend to require, and therefore develop, more arbitrators. The process then comes closer to fulfilling its promise of speed and low-cost resolution. And in the 1980s, the parties have developed considerably more expertise and sophistication in the formulation and administration of labor agreements. It is wholly appropriate, under such circumstances, that the arbitrator be required to confine himself to the more technical role of interpreting the agreement.

Yet, it would be myopic for one to lose sight of the basic differences between dispute resolution in this context as opposed to that of the courts'. The fundamental distinction, of course, is that the parties to the labor relationship must continue to work together. As observed at the outset of this volume, breach of the labor agreement leads not to its dissolution but instead to a remedy that permits continuation of the relationship. That single fact demands an extra measure of thoughtful attention in the handling of disputes. It is that unique factor that makes the system vulnerable to the onset of litigation techniques. Yet, this is precisely the challenge now faced by the system.

Increasingly, parties are inclined toward courtroom atmospheres. The lower steps of the grievance procedure, designed and intended to be dispute-settling mechanisms, are increasingly viewed as mere discovery vehicles. Unions are less willing to settle matters for fear of fair representation suits, and management, for its part, is increasingly concerned about undercutting the authority of the supervisor on the line; as bureaucracies enlarge, settlement becomes more elusive.

The natural result of a system that leans more toward ad hoc arbitration, outside representatives, and increasing reliance upon external law is that the fundamental value of labor arbitration will be ignored and finally irretrievably lost. The process has flourished and gained broad acceptability because of its unique ability to be custom-tailored to the needs of the individual parties and their labor agreement.

The parties have not been unaware of the need for sensitivity in this respect. In 1978, National Academy of Arbitrators President Arthur Stark discussed the numerous innovative and flexible measures incorporated by parties in the steel, auto, rubber, and construction industries. He also reviewed experiments in expedited procedures in brewery, fabricating, airline, and broadcasting industries. Several industries, including the bituminous coal, publishing, railroads, and public sector, had adopted appellate and quasi-appellate procedures. And interest arbitration had been utilized in the transportation and hotel industries as well as in the public sector in various contexts. Professional sports and governmental agencies were adopting new arbitration systems as well. These are signs of health and continued vitality. They ought to be studied and, when appropriate, emulated.

There is, then, no end to any so-called "golden age" of arbitration. But there is an increasing danger of allowing this unique and important process to become little more than a mere legal forum. It is capable of far more than that, and the continued recognition of this fact by both the neutrals and the parties is essential.

Suggested Readings

Chapter 2

Chamberlain, "Collective Bargaining and the Concept of Contract," 48 *Colum. L. Rev.* 829 (1948).

"Customs and Usages as Factors in Arbitration Decisions," *NYU 15th Annual Conference on Labor* (New York: Matthew Bender, 1962).

Doyle, "Past Practice as Standard in Arbitration," 39 *Personnel* 66 (1962).

Elkouri & Elkouri, *How Arbitration Works*, 3d ed. (Washington, D.C.: BNA Books, 1973), at 296–320.

Fairweather, *Practice and Procedure in Labor Arbitration* (Washington, D.C.: BNA Books, 1973), at Chap. 10.

Feinsinger, "Enforcement of Labor Agreements—A New Era in Collective Bargaining," 43 *Va. L. Rev.* 1261 (1957).

Feller, "A General Theory of the Collective Bargaining Agreement," 61 *Calif. L. Rev.* 663 (1973).

Feller, *Labor Law Developments 1967*, Proceedings of the 13th Annual Institute on Labor Law 1 (Dallas, Tex.: Southwestern Legal Foundation, 1967).

Fleming, "Reflections on the Nature of Labor Arbitration," 61 *Mich. L. Rev.* 1245 (1963).

Fleming, "Some Observations on Contract Grievances Before Courts and Arbitrators," 15 *Stan. L. Rev.* 595 (1963).

Garrett, "The Role of Lawyers in Arbitration," *Arbitration and Public Policy*, Proceedings of the 14th Annual Meeting, National Academy of Arbitrators (Washington, D.C.: BNA Books, 1961), at 102.

Gillman, "Past Practice in the Administration of Collective Bargaining Agreements in Arbitration," 4 *Suffolk U.L. Rev.* 689 (1970).

Gregory, "The Law of the Collective Agreement," 57 *Mich. L. Rev.* 635 (1959).

Killingsworth, "Arbitration: Its Uses in Industrial Relations," 21 *L.A.* 859 (1953).

Marceau, "Are All Interpretations Admissible?" 12 *Arb. J.* 150 (1957).

Mittenthal, "Past Practice and the Administration of Collective Bargaining Agreements," *Arbitration and Public Policy,* Proceedings of the 14th Annual Meeting, National Academy of Arbitrators (Washington, D.C.: BNA Books, 1961), at 30.

Mueller, "The Law of Contracts—A Changing Legal Environment," *Truth, Lie Detectors, and Other Problems in Labor Arbitration,* Proceedings of the 31st Annual Meeting, National Academy of Arbitrators (Washington, D.C.: BNA Books, 1979), at 204.

Shulman, "Reason, Contract and Law in Labor Relations," 68 *Harv. L. Rev.* 999 (1955).

Summers, "Collective Agreements and the Law of Contract," 98 *Yale L.J.* 525 (1969).

Treece, "Past Practice and Its Relationship to Specific Contract Language in the Arbitration of Grievance Disputes," 40 *U. Colo. L. Rev.* 358 (1968).

Trotta, "Contract Interpretation," *Arbitration of Labor Management Disputes* (New York: Amacon, 1974).

Wallen, "The Silent Contract vs. Express Provisions: The Arbitration of Local Working Conditions," *Collective Bargaining and the Arbitrator's Role,* Proceedings of the 15th Annual Meeting, National Academy of Arbitrators (Washington, D.C.: BNA Books, 1962), at 117.

Witmer, "Collective Labor Agreements in the Courts," 48 *Yale L.J.* 195 (1938).

Yaffe, *The Saul Wallen Papers: A Neutral's Contribution to Industrial Peace* (Ithaca, New York: NY School of Labor and Industrial Relations, Cornell U., 1974).

Youngdahl, "Judicial Review of Labor Arbitration Awards Which Rely on the Practices of the Parties," 65 *Mich. L. Rev.* 1647 (1967).

Zack, *Understanding Grievance Arbitration in the Public Sector* (Washington, D.C.: U.S. Department of Labor, 1980), at Chaps. X and XI.

Chapter 3

Aksen, "Post-Gardner-Denver Developments in Arbitration Law," *Arbitration—1975,* Proceedings of the 28th Annual Meeting, National Academy of Arbitrators (Washington, D.C.: BNA Books, 1976), at 24.

Baroni, "The Effect of Title VII of the 1964 Civil Rights Act Upon Arbitration," 9 *Bus. L. Rev.* 11 (1976).

Bloch, "Labor Arbitration's Crossroads Revisited: The Role of the Arbitrator and the Response of the Courts," 47 *U. Cin. L. Rev.* 363 (1978).

Block, "Legal and Traditional Criteria in Arbitration of Sexual Discrimination Grievances," 32 *Arb. J.* 241 (1977).

Blumrosen, "Individual Worker-Employer Arbitration Under Title VII," 31 *NYU Conf. on Lab.* 329 (1978).

Clarke, "Substantial Evidence and Labor Arbitration in the Federal Sector," 31 *Lab. L.J.* 368 (1980).

Coleman, "The Civil Service Reform Act of 1978: Its Meaning and Its Roots," 31 *Lab. L.J.* 200 (1980).

Cooper, "Gardner-Denver: The View from EEOC," 27 *NYU Conf. on Lab.* 183 (1974).

Cooper & Bauer, "Federal Sector Labor Relations Reform," 56 *Chi.-Kent L. Rev.* 509 (1980).

Coulson, "Another Seat at the Table: Gardner-Denver, 1974," 27 *NYU Conf. on Lab.* 190 (1974).

Coulson, "Black Alice in Gardner-Denverland," *Arbitration—1974,* Proceedings of the 27th Annual Meeting, National Academy of Arbitrators (Washington, D.C.: BNA Books, 1975), at 236.

Edwards, "Arbitration of Employment Discrimination Cases: An Empirical Study," *Arbitration—1975,* Proceedings of the 28th Annual Meeting, National Academy of Arbitrators (Washington, D.C.: BNA Books, 1976), at 59.

Edwards, "Labor Arbitration at the Crossroads—The Common Law of the Shop v. External Law," 32 *Arb. J.* 65 (1977).

Elkouri & Elkouri, *How Arbitration Works,* 3d ed., suppl. "Legal Status of Federal Sector Arbitration" (Washington, D.C.: BNA Books, 1980).

Ferris, "Remedies in Federal Sector Promotion Grievances," 34 *Arb. J.* 37 (1979).

Frazier, "Labor Arbitration in the Federal Service," 45 *Geo. Wash. L. Rev.* 372 (1977).

Gamser, "Back-Seat Driving Behind the Back-Seat Driver: Arbitration in the Federal Sector," *Truth, Lie Detectors, and Other Problems in Labor Arbitration*, Proceedings of the 31st Annual Meeting, National Academy of Arbitrators (Washington, D.C.: BNA Books, 1979), at 268.

Hill, "Authority of Labor Arbitrators to Decide Legal Issues Under Collective Bargaining Contracts: The Situation After Alexander v. Gardner-Denver," 10 *Ind. L. Rev.* 899 (1977).

Jacobs, "Confusion Remains Five Years After Alexander v. Gardner-Denver," 30 *Lab. L.J.* 623 (1979).

Jones, "The Role of Arbitration in State and National Labor Policy," *Arbitration and the Public Interest*, Proceedings of the 24th Annual Meeting, National Academy of Arbitrators (Washington, D.C.: BNA Books, 1971), at 42.

Kagel, "Grievance Arbitration in the Federal Sector: How Final and Binding," 51 *Or. L. Rev.* 134 (1971).

Kagel, "Grievance Arbitration in the Federal Service: Still Hardly Final and Binding," 914 *Govt. Emp. Rel. Rep.* 31 (1981).

Linsey, "Federal Sector Grievance Arbitration Under the Civil Service Reform Act of 1978," 21 *Air Force L. Rev.* 376 (1979).

Meltzer, "The Impact of Gardner-Denver on Labor Arbitration," 27 *NYU Conf. on Lab.* 201 (1974).

Murphy, "Impact of ERISA on Arbitration," 32 *Arb. J.* 123 (1977).

Murphy, "Title VII Filing Period and Arbitration: Is Culpepper v. Reynolds Metal Co. Still Good Law?" 27 *Syracuse L. Rev.* 1163 (1976).

Nauman, "Post-Gardner-Denver Developments in the Arbitration of Discrimination Claims," *Arbitration—1975*, Proceedings of the 28th Annual Meeting, National Academy of Arbitrators (Washington, D.C.: BNA Books, 1976), at 36.

Nesbitt, *Labor Relations in the Federal Government Service* (Washington, D.C.: BNA Books, 1976).

Note, "Alexander v. Gardner-Denver, and Deferral to Labor Arbitration," 27 *Hast. L.J.* 483 (1975).

Note, "False Hope of a Footnote: Arbitration of Title VII Disputes After Alexander v. Gardner-Denver," 8 *Loy. U. Chi. L.J.* 847 (1977).

Note, "Federal Employment—The Civil Service Reform Act of 1978—Removing Incompetency and Protecting Whistle Blowers," 26 *Wayne L. Rev.* 97 (1979).

Note, "Federal Sector Arbitration Under the Civil Service Reform Act of 1978," 17 *San Diego L. Rev.* 857 (1980).

Porter, "Arbitration in the Federal Government: What Happened to the 'Magna Carta'?" *Arbitration—1977,* Proceedings of the 30th Annual Meeting, National Academy of Arbitrators (Washington, D.C.: BNA Books, 1978), at 90.

Richards, "Alexander v. Gardner-Denver: A Threat to Title VII Rights?" 29 *Ark. L. Rev.* 129 (1975).

Rosenberg, "Sex Discrimination and the Labor Arbitration Process," 30 *Lab. L.J.* 102 (1979).

Smith, "Title VII of the Civil Service Reform Act of 1978: A 'Perfect' Order?" 31 *Hast. L.J.* 855 (1980).

Sovern, "When Should Arbitrators Follow Federal Law?" *Arbitration and the Expanding Role of Neutrals,* Proceedings of the 23rd Annual Meeting, National Academy of Arbitrators (Washington, D.C.: BNA Books, 1970), at 29.

St. Antoine, "Judicial Review of Labor Arbitration Awards," 75 *Mich. L. Rev.* 1137 (1977).

Sulzner, "The Impact of Grievance and Arbitration Processes on Federal Personnel Policies and Practices: The View From Twenty Bargaining Units," 9 *J. of Col. Negot. in the Public Sector* 143 (1980) (873 *Govt. Emp. Rel. Rep.* 8, 1980).

Webster, "Arbitration of the Title VII Disputes: A Proposal," 33 *Arb. J.* 25 (1970).

Wolfson, "Social Policy and Title VII Arbitration," 68 *Ky. L.J.* 101 (1980).

Young, "The Authority and Obligation of a Labor Arbitrator to Modify or Eliminate a Provision of a Collective Bargaining Agreement Because in His Opinion It Violated Federal Law," 32 *Ohio St. L.J.* 395 (1971).

Zack, "Education in the External Law: Training Who, How, For What?" *Dispute Settlement Training* (New York: American Arbitration Association, 1978), at 51.

Zatzkis, "Arbitral Deferral Under Title VII, NLRA and FLSA After Alexander v. Gardner-Denver," 22 *La. B. J.* 99 (1974).

Chapter 4

Bairstow, "New Dimensions in Public-Sector Grievance Arbitration," *Truth, Lie Detectors, and Other Problems in Labor Arbitration,* Proceedings of the 31st Annual Meeting, National Academy of Arbitrators (Washington, D.C.: BNA Books, 1979), at 232.

Chamberlain, "The Union's Challenge to Management Control," 16 *Ind. & Lab. Rel. Rev.* 184 (1963).

Chamberlain, "Work Assignments and Industrial Change," *Labor Arbitration: Perspectives and Problems,* Proceedings of the 17th Annual Meeting, National Academy of Arbitrators (Washington, D.C.: BNA Books, 1964), at 224.

Chandler, *Management Rights and Union Interests* (New York: McGraw-Hill, 1964).

Goldberg, "Management's Reserved Rights: A Labor View," *Management Rights and the Arbitration Process,* Proceedings of the 9th Annual Meeting, National Academy of Arbitrators (Washington, D. C.: BNA Books, 1956), at 118.

Horlacher, "Employee Job Rights Versus Employer Job Control: The Arbitrator's Choice," *Collective Bargaining and the Arbitrator's Role,* Proceedings of the 15th Annual Meeting, National Academy of Arbitrators (Washington, D.C.: BNA Books, 1962), at 165.

Justin, *Management Rights and the Arbitration Process* (Washington, D.C.: BNA Books, 1956).

Killingsworth, "The Presidential Address: Management Rights Revisited," *Arbitration and Social Change,* Proceedings of the 22nd Annual Meeting, National Academy of Arbitrators (Washington, D.C.: BNA Books, 1970), at 1.

McManus, "Rights to Manage is Caught up in the Arbitration Crosswinds," 192 *Iron Age* 41 (1956).

Ostrin, "Reserved Rights in Arbitration," *NYU 12th Annual Conference on Labor* (New York: Matthew Bender, 1959).

Phelps, "Management's Reserved Rights: An Industry View," *Management Rights and the Arbitration Process,* Proceedings of the 9th Annual Meeting, National Academy of Arbitrators (Washington, D.C.: BNA Books, 1956), at 102.

Platt, *Labor Relations Yearbook, 1968* (Washington, D.C: BNA Books, 1969), at 145.

Prawson & Peters, "New Perspectives on Management Reserved Rights," 18 *Lab. L.J.* 3 (1967).

Rubin, "Right of Management to Split Jobs and Assign Work to Other Jobs," 16 *Ind. & Lab. Rel. Rev.* 205 (1963).

Seward, "Arbitration and Functions of Management," 16 *Ind. & Lab. Rel. Rev.* 235 (1963).

Stein, "Management Rights and Productivity," 32 *Arb. J.* 270 (1977).

Stone, *Managerial Freedom and Job Security* (New York: Harper & Row, 1962).

Torrance, *Management's Right to Manage* (Washington, D.C.: BNA Books, 1968).

Updegraff, *Arbitration and Labor Relations*, 3d ed. (Washington, D.C.: BNA Books, 1970), at 362.

Young, "The Question of Managerial Prerogative," 16 *Ind. & Lab. Rel. Rev.* 24 (1963).

Chapter 5

Christensen, "The Disguised Review of the Merits of Arbitration Awards," *Labor Arbitration at the Quarter-Century Mark*, Proceedings of the 25th Annual Meeting, National Academy of Arbitrators (Washington, D.C.: BNA Books, 1973), at 99.

Cohen, "Gardner-Denver Decision and Labor Arbitration," 27 *Lab. L.J.* 18 (1976).

Cornfield, "Developing Standards for Determining Arbitrability," 14 *Lab. L.J.* 564 (1963).

Elkouri & Elkouri, *How Arbitration Works*, 3d ed. (Washington, D.C.: BNA Books, 1973), at 169.

Fairweather, *Practice and Procedure in Labor Arbitration* (Washington, D.C.: BNA Books, 1973), at Chap. 6.

Fleming, "Arbitration and Arbitrability," 104 *Wash. U.L.Q.* 200 (1963).

Galgani, "Judicial Review of Arbitrability of Arbitration Awards in the Public Sector," 19 *Santa Clara L. Rev.* 937 (1978).

Jones, *"The Name of the Game is Decision—Some Reflections on Arbitrability and Authority in Labor Relations,"* 46 *Texas L. Rev.* 865 (1968).

Jones et al., "Arbitration and Rights Under Collective Agreements," *Problems of Proof in Arbitration*, Proceedings of the 19th Annual Meeting, National Academy of Arbitrators (Washington, D.C.: BNA Books, 1967), at 366.

Justin, "Arbitrability and the Arbitration Jurisdiction," *Management Rights and the Arbitration Process*, Proceedings of the 9th Annual Meeting, National Academy of Arbitrators (Washington, D.C.: BNA Books, 1956), at 1.

McDermott, "Arbitrability; the Courts vs. the Arbitrator," 23 *Arb. J.* 18 (1968).

Note, "Judicial Review of Labor Arbitration Awards After the Trilogy," 53 *Cornell L. Rev.* 136 (1967).

Note, "Labor Law—Arbitrability—In Course Termination of Collective Bargaining Agreement Presents Issue for Judicial Resolution," 43 *Fordham L. Rev.* 880 (1975).

Note, "Labor Law—Arbitration—Dispute Involving Hazardous Working Conditions is Within the Scope of Broad Arbitration Clause of Collective Bargaining Agreement in Absence of Forceful Indication of Exclusionary Intent," 7 *Akron L. Rev.* 508 (1974).

Note, "Presumption of Arbitrability Applies to Safety Disputes," 28 *Ark. L. Rev.* 498 (1975).

Pirsig, "Arbitrability and the Uniform Act," 19 *Arb. J.* 154 (1964).

Rains, "Boys Market Injunctions: Strict Scrutiny of the Presumption of Arbitrability," 28 *Hast L.J.* 30 (1976).

Smith, "Arbitrators and Arbitrability," *Labor Arbitration and Industrial Change,* Proceedings of the 16th Annual Meeting, National Academy of Arbitrators (Washington, D.C.: BNA Books, 1963), at 75.

Smith & Jones, "The Impact of the Emerging Federal Law of Grievance Arbitration on Judges, Arbitrators and Parties," 52 *Va. L. Rev.* 831 (1966).

Smith & Jones, "The Supreme Court and Labor Dispute Arbitration: The Emerging Federal Law," 64 *Mich. L. Rev.* 751 (1965).

Taleise, "Search for Arbitrability Formulas in Contract of NY Teachers," 30 *Arb. J.* 114 (1975).

Vaccaro, "Significance of Recent Decisions on Grievance Arbitrability Questions in Public Sector Labor Relations," 83 *J. of Law & Educ.* 379 (1979).

Chapter 6

Comment, "Title VII and Seniority Systems: Back to the Foot on the Line?" 64 *Ky. L.J.* 487 (1975).

Cooper & Sobol, "Seniority and Testing Under Fair Employment Law," 82 *Harv. L. Rev.* 1598 (1969).

Gould, "Employment Security, Seniority and Race, the Role of Title VII in the Civil Rights Act of 1964," 13 *How. L.J.* 1 (1967).

Meltzer & Kohrs, "Tests and the Requirement of the Jobs," 20 *Arb. J.* 103 (1965).

Note, "Employment Discrimination and Title VII of the Civil Rights Act of 1964," 84 *Harv. L. Rev.* 1109 (1971).

Note, "Seniority and Equal Employment Opportunity," 23 *Rutgers L. Rev.* 268 (1969).

Note, "Title VII: Seniority Discrimination and the Incumbent Negro," 80 *Harv. L. Rev.* 1260 (1967).

Note, "Use of Tests in Promotion Under Seniority Provision," 21 *Vand. L. Rev.* 100–124 (1967).

Silbergold, "Title VII and the Collective Bargaining Agreement: Seniority Provisions Under Fire," 49 *Temple L.Q.* 288 (1976).

Chapter 7

Aaron, "Discussion: The Arbitration of Discharge Cases," *Critical Issues in Labor Arbitration,* Proceedings of the 10th Annual Meeting, National Academy of Arbitrators (Washington, D.C.: BNA Books, 1957), at 17.

Abrams, "Theory for the Discharge Case," 36 *Arb J.* 24 (1981).

Atleson, "Disciplinary Discharge Arbitration and NLRB Deference," 20 *Buff. L. Rev.* 358 (1977).

Baer, "Arbitrating the Discharge and Discipline of Union Officials," 91 *Monthly L. Rev.* 39 (1969).

Bailer, "The Discipline Issue in Arbitration: Individual Differences and Shop Practices," 15 *Lab. L.J.* 567 (1964).

Benewitz, "Discharge Arbitration and the Quantum of Proof," 28 *Arb. J.* 95 (1978).

Bernstein, *Remedies in Labor Arbitration* (Washington, D.C.: BNA Books, 1960).

Comment, "Labor Law—Authority of Arbitrator to Determine Remedy for Violation of the Collective Bargaining Agreement," 43 *Marq. L. Rev.* 260 (1959).

Davey, "The Arbitrator Speaks on Discharge and Discipline," 17 *Arb. J.* 97 (1962).

Fairweather, *Practice and Procedure in Labor Arbitration* (Washington, D.C.: BNA Books, 1973).

Fallon, "The Discipline and Discharge Case: Two Devil's Advocates on What Arbitrators Are Doing Wrong," *Arbitration of Subcontracting and Wage Incentive Disputes,* Proceedings of the 32nd Annual Meeting, National Academy of Arbitrators (Washington, D.C.: BNA Books, 1980), at 82.

Feller, "Remedies in Arbitration: The Power of the Arbitrator to Make Monetary Awards," *Labor Arbitration: Perspectives and Problems,* Proceedings of the 17th Annual Meeting, National Academy of Arbitrators (Washington, D.C.: BNA Books, 1964), at 193.

Ferris, "Remedies in Federal Sector Promotion Grievances," 34 *Arb. J.* 37 (1979).

Fischbach, "Past Misconduct in Discharge Cases," 24 *Arb. J.* 175 (1969).

Fisher, "Ramifications of Back Pay in Suspension and Discharge Cases," *Arbitration and Social Change*, Proceedings of the 22nd Annual Meeting, National Academy of Arbitrators (Washington, D.C.: BNA Books, 1970), at 175.

Fleming, "Arbitrators and the Remedy Power," 48 *Va. L. Rev.* 1199 (1962).

Gilroy, "Deferred Discipline: Wrinkle or Facelifting?" 20 *Lab. L.J.* 47 (1969).

Handsaker, "Remedies and Penalties for Wildcat Strikes: How Arbitrators and Federal Courts Have Ruled," 22 *Cath. U. L. Rev.* 279 (1973).

Heath, "Defining the Issue and the Remedy," *The Arbitrator, the NLRB, and the Courts*, Proceedings of the 20th Annual Meeting, National Academy of Arbitrators (Washington, D.C.: BNA Books, 1967), at 352.

Holly, "The Arbitration of Discharge Cases: A Case Study," *Critical Issues in Labor Arbitration*, Proceedings of the 10th Annual Meeting, National Academy of Arbitrators (Washington, D.C.: BNA Books, 1957), at 1.

Jennings, "Discharge Cases Reconsidered," 31 *Arb. J.* 164 (1976).

Jones, *Arbitration and Industrial Discipline* (Ann Arbor, Mich.: Bureau of Industrial Relations, 1961).

Jones, "Ramifications of Back-Pay Awards in Suspension and Discharge Cases," *Arbitration and Social Change*, Proceedings of the 22nd Annual Meeting, National Academy of Arbitrators (Washington, D.C.: BNA Books, 1970), at 163.

Kerr, "The New Opportunities for Industrial Relations," *Arbitration and Public Policy*, Proceedings of the 14th Annual Meeting, National Academy of Arbitrators (Washington, D.C.: BNA Books, 1961), at 184.

Lazar, "Notes on Discharge for Causes," 92 *Wash. U. L.Q.* 196 (1949).

Miller, "The Discipline and Discharge Case: Two Devil's Advocates on What Arbitrators Are Doing Wrong," *Arbitration of Subcontracting and Wage Incentive Disputes*, Proceedings of the 32nd Annual Meeting, National Academy of Arbitrators (Washington, D.C.: BNA Books, 1980), at 75.

Myers, "Concepts of Industrial Discipline," *Management Rights and the Arbitration Process*, Proceedings of 9th Annual Meeting, National Academy of Arbitrators (Washington, D.C.: BNA Books, 1956), at 59.

Note, "Arbitration in Discharge Cases," 91 *Monthly Lab. Rev.* 1 (1968).

Note, "Remedial Authority of the Labour Arbitrator: A Postscript," 15 *Osgoode Hall L.J.* 25 (1977).

Phelps, *Discipline and Discharge in the Unionized Firm* (Berkeley, Calif.: University of California Press, 1959).

Ross, "The Arbitration of Discharge Cases: What Happens After Reinstatement," *Critical Issues in Labor Arbitration*, Proceedings of the 10th Annual Meeting, National Academy of Arbitrators (Washington, D.C.: BNA Books, 1957), at 21.

Seitz, "Problems of the Finality of Awards, or Functus Officio and All That," *Labor Arbitration: Perspectives and Problems*, Proceedings of the 17th Annual Meeting, National Academy of Arbitrators (Washington, D.C.: BNA Books, 1964), at 165.

Seitz, "Substitution of Disciplinary Suspension for Discharge: A Proposed Guide to the Perplexed in Arbitration," 35 *Arb. J.* 27 (1980).

Sirefman, "Rights Without Remedies in Labor Arbitration," 19 *Arb. J.* 17 (1963).

Somers, "Alcohol and the Just Cause for Discharge," *Arbitration—1975*, Proceedings of the 28th Annual Meeting, National Academy of Arbitrators (Washington, D.C.: BNA Books, 1976), at 103.

Stein, "Remedies in Labor Arbitration," *Challenges to Arbitration*, Proceedings of the 13th Annual Meeting, National Academy of Arbitrators (Washington, D.C.: BNA Books, 1960), at 39.

Stessin, *Employee Discipline* (Washington, D.C.: BNA Books, 1960).

Stutz, "Arbitrators and the Remedy Power," *Labor Arbitration and Industrial Change*, Proceedings of the 16th Annual Meeting, National Academy of Arbitrators (Washington, D.C.: BNA Books, 1963), at 54.

Teple, "Discipline and Discharge at the Arbitration Level," 6 *Law Notes* 79 (1970).

Trotta, *Arbitration of Labor Management Disputes* (New York: Amacon, 1974), at 231.

Weiler, "Remedial Authority of the Labour Arbitrator: Revised Judicial Version," 52 *Canadian Bar Rev.* 29 (1974).

Wolff, "The Power of the Arbitrator to Make Monetary Awards," *Labor Arbitration: Perspectives and Problems*, Proceedings of the 17th Annual Meeting, National Academy of Arbitrators (Washington, D.C.: BNA Books, 1964), at 176.

Wynns, "Arbitration Standards in Dru Discharge Cases," 54 *Arb. J.* 19 (1979).

Youngdahl, "Awarding Interest in Labor Arbitration Cases," 54 *Ky. L.J.* 717 (1966).

Zack & Bloch, *The Arbitration of Discipline Cases* (New York: American Arbitration Association, 1979).

Chapter 8

Code of Federal Regulations, "Questions and Answers on the Pregnancy Discrimination Act," Pub. L. No. 95-555, 29 C.F.R. §1604 (1978).

Elkouri & Elkouri, *How Arbitration Works*, 3d ed. (Washington, D.C.: BNA Books, 1973), at 680.

Hill, "Reasonable Accommodation and Religious Discrimination Under Title VII: A Practitioner's Guide," 34 *Arb. J.* 19 (No. 4), (1979).

Note, "Bargaining Obligations of Successor Employers," 88 *Stan. L. Rev.* 759 (1975).

Note, "Employee Rights in Mergers and Takeovers: EEC Proposals and the American Approach," 25 *International and Comp. L.Q.* 621 (1976).

Rothschild, Merrifield, & Edwards, *Collective Bargaining and Labor Arbitration* (New York: Bobbs Merrill, 1979), at 690, 698.

Wolkinson, "Title VII and the Religious Employee," 30 *Arb. J.* 89 (1979).

Index